Instant Pot®
Miracle
HEALTHY
COOKBOOK

Instant Pot® Miracle

Miracle

HEALTHY

COOKBOOK

More Than 100 Easy Healthy Meals
for Your Favorite Kitchen Device

URVASHI PITRE

PHOTOGRAPHY BY GHAZALLE BADIOZAMANI

HOUGHTON MIFFLIN HARCOURT

BOSTON NEW YORK 2021

For information about permission to reproduce selections from this book, write to trade.permissions@hmhco.com or to Permissions, Houghton Mifflin Harcourt Publishing Company, 3 Park Avenue, 19th Floor, New York, New York 10016.

hmhbooks.com

Library of Congress Cataloging-in-Publication Data is available.

ISBN 978-0-358-41318-9 (pbk)

ISBN 987-0-358-41477-3 (ebk)

Book design by Jennifer K. Beal Davis

Printed in China

SCP 10 9 8 7 6 5 4 3 2 1

To my husband, Roger,
who is my best friend
and my staunchest advocate.
I couldn't do any of this
without you.

CONTENTS

BEEF, PORK, AND LAMB

SEAFOOD

LENTILS, BEANS, AND LEGUMES

RICE AND GRAINS

SAUCES AND SPICE MIXES

ACKNOWLEDGMENTS

My biggest thanks go to my fans, followers, and readers, who continue to support, suggest, encourage, and make me laugh daily. If it weren't for you, I'd be creating recipes that absolutely no one made—and how little fun would that be?

My husband, who continues to eat all my successes and failures and gives me honest feedback no matter what.

Sheila Ward, who helped me painstakingly test every recipe in this book, some of them more than once.

Sammy and Paul Brakebill and Ashley Reachelle, who help me keep TwoSleevers.com going when I'm in the throes of recipe creation.

Lisa Kingsley and Will Bortz, for rewriting the recipes for clarity.

My agent, Stacey Glick, who is always available when I need her and who supports me in so many ways.

My editor, Justin Schwartz, whose involvement and input really help these books come together.

Ghazalle Badiozamani and her team of accomplished stylists and helpers, who make my food look pretty—not just tasty. Thank you to Monica Pierini, Jenna Tedesco, and Bridget Kenny for your great work. I so love working with you.

Thanks also to Bridget Nocera and Samantha Simon, who help me brainstorm crazy marketing and publicity ideas, as well as the whole army at Houghton Mifflin Harcourt, who helped, without my even realizing it, to make this book a reality.

WHAT DOES *HEALTHY* EVEN MEAN?

Good question! I debated the title of this book so much because healthy means different things to different people. I cannot imagine that a vegan and a carnivore keto person could ever agree on all points of healthy eating. I myself have been vegetarian as well as keto over the years, and I'd be the last person to tell you that one way of eating is good for everyone.

What I did was select criteria that I think most people would agree constitute healthy, nourishing food.

- **Every recipe is under 500 calories.** When you add other side dishes, your meal will probably be higher in total calories, but I did my part by keeping calories low without sacrificing taste.
- **Whole unprocessed food.** If you've followed me on my blog, TwoSleevers.com, or bought any of my other cookbooks, you know that I almost never use packaged mixes and canned soups. You won't find any cream-of-anything recipes in this book, either. As much as possible, I used whole, unprocessed foods.
- **Minimal or no processed and refined carbs such as flour and sugar.** Carbs are included in these recipes, but they are carbs from whole, unprocessed ingredients such as beans, grains, and vegetables. I included one or two pasta recipes just so you'd know how to cook them if you wanted, but they are the exception, not the norm.
- **A balance of carbs and fat.** If a recipe was high in carbs, I tried to ensure it was low in fat, since most of us are trying to eat either less fat or fewer carbs, but not both of those at the same time.
- **Dietary substitutions.** I suggested substitutions for vegan, dairy-free, and lower-carb diets throughout the book when possible. If you're trying to increase fat in your diet, you don't need me to tell you how easy it is to do that! Add cheese, sub out half-and-half for evaporated milk, use full-fat dairy products as garnishes, and add even more cheese! For dairy-free/vegan options, I've suggested oil instead of ghee or butter,

and coconut milk instead of evaporated milk. If you use vegan cheese, that would open up many other recipes for you to try.

- **Minimal or no added sweeteners, both natural and artificial.** A few of the recipes suggest a pinch of sugar or sweetener as optional. Sometimes a recipe needs a touch of sweetness to counteract the acid, but this is purely optional in all the recipes in this book.

- **High-fiber vegetables.** You will notice that I call for a lot of veggies in these recipes. While that increases the number of ingredients, your mother was right when she said veggies were good for you! They also happen to be super-tasty when done right. Their colorful appearance also tends to make eating with your eyes that much easier, so enjoy all the vegetables.

- **Meat as a seasoning.** You may look at some of these recipes and wonder why I think a pound of meat should feed six people. It will make sense if you consider the fact that the recipe also calls for lots of veggies. In this case, meat serves as an important, but not central, part of the meal. If you're looking for additional vegetarian recipes, you might be interested in my *Instant Pot Miracle Vegetarian Cookbook* as well.

- **Minimal processed meats.** I love bacon and sausages as much as the next girl. But since many of us try to reduce or avoid nitrates and processed meats, I only have one or two recipes that use bacon or smoked sausage. Everything else calls for fresh meats and often naturally lean meats.

There you have it. In the context of this book, *healthy* means lower calories, minimal processed ingredients, mostly whole foods, and recipes that are rich with vegetables.

One last note: I am not a trained chef. I am, like most of you, a home cook. I have a lot of experience in making meals for my family in between meetings or during conference calls (Hey, don't judge! We all do it!), so my recipes are simple—but flavorful.

As I said earlier, there's no one definition of healthy, but I do think that homemade food is easier to make healthy than eating out, so I am all in favor of cooking and eating at home! My goal is to give you recipes that are easy to make, taste good, and make you a hero in the eyes of your fellow diners, including the littlest (and often most whiny!) ones. If you can chop, measure, stir, and blend, you can make any of the recipes in this book. In other words, you've got no excuse for not making healthy food anymore.

Here's to good health and good eating for us all.

INTRODUCTION

I have been cooking with pressure cookers for more than thirty-five years. (I feel old just writing that! Let's just assume I started cooking at two years old, okay?) My relationship with them has evolved. Just as in other long-term relationships, over the years I have loved them, used them, taken them for granted during busy times, explored their capabilities during times of rest, understood their giving nature better, and fallen in love with them again.

About five years ago, I discovered the world of electric pressure cookers. Soon after, the Instant Pot entered my life, and slowly it took over my kitchen. In fact, as my life was taken over by a degenerative disease that often limited my mobility, I began to rely more and more on these devices that allowed me to cook a quick, nutritious dinner without babysitting, standing, stirring, and mixing.

My husband, Roger, and I were also on a weight-loss journey, and home-cooked meals were critical in this endeavor. Together, we have lost and kept off about 175 pounds, and cooking healthy meals at home was an important part of how we accomplished this feat.

My son, Mark, learned to cook with a pressure cooker when he was nineteen years old. I still remember when he mastered four different dishes in one day. Now Mark is scary-smart, this is true, but it's also true that pressure cookers are not that complicated.

I want to use this book, my blog (twosleevers.com), and my Facebook groups as a way to introduce you to the delights of cooking in a pressure cooker. I assure you, once you realize all that it can do, you may well find the other appliances in your kitchen, along with your stove, becoming sorely neglected.

If you are a novice cook, forget all your fears, your concerns, and your confusion. Just pick a recipe from this book—any recipe—and make it by following the simple directions. Through the pages of this book, I'll help you create amazing meals. Just like the thousands before you who never cooked but now make my recipes nightly, you, too, can do this. If you are an accomplished cook already, you may enjoy the different shortcuts I use as well as appreciate the wide range of flavors and cuisines covered in this book.

There's something for everyone in this recipe book. I hope you enjoy it. If you run into issues, do be sure to ask me questions on my blog, twosleevers.com, or come join my TwoSleevers Facebook group, facebook.com/twosleevers, which is filled with helpful, kind folks ready to lend a hand.

THE RECIPES IN THIS BOOK

Very Easy

If you can chop, mix, blend, stir, and press buttons, you can make these recipes. Yes, your fourteen-year-old can likely make most of this food. They were designed to be easy for the average home chef—you know, the real people like me who don't have caviar, octopus, and that certain truffle that only grows in the Alps just lying around in their pantry. Many of these recipes use pantry and freezer vegetables but not canned cream-of-anything soups or ready-made sauces in cans. Having said that, I do like to cook recipes from around the world. There are recipes that may call for ingredients you don't currently have.

Authentic Recipes from Around the World

You may not be familiar with all the cuisines and taste profiles I feature in this book. Here's your chance to try something different while relying on recipes that are extremely well tested and whose flavors have been blessed by those who grew up eating or cooking these recipes from around the world. My very active Facebook group is filled with foodies, many of whom are well traveled and accomplished cooks. They helped vet the ease and authenticity of all of these recipes.

I urge you to step out of your usual cooking rut or your comfort zone with some of these recipes, and do so with the expectation that you and your family may find flavors that become your new favorites. My advice to you is don't tell yourself, "Oh, but I don't like [insert cuisine here]." Rather, look at a recipe and its ingredients. Does it have flavors you enjoy? If so, try making the recipe. Nine times out of ten, my readers who do this end up raving about a hitherto unheard-of dish. Of course, if you hate mushrooms, you're unlikely to enjoy them in any dish, no matter what the cuisine. So be a little brave, but use what you know about your tastes to pick and choose.

Thoroughly Tested

Every recipe in this book has been tested not just by me but by several people in my TwoSleevers Facebook group, as well as by readers of my blog. Make each recipe once as written and then feel free to experiment. What this means is that if a recipe doesn't work for you, it's unlikely to be the recipe and more likely to be something that you could do differently. If a recipe doesn't work for you, please ask questions on my blog or in my Facebook group and someone will help you.

I tested (and retested!) all the Instant Pot recipes in either a six-quart Duo, six-quart Ultra, or three-quart Mini Instant Pot. Each model has its own nuances, so I've tried to keep the instructions as generic as possible. These recipes work as written in a six-quart Instant Pot. All but the ones that require pot-in-pot cooking or that cook more than a pound of meat at a time also work in a three-quart model. If you're using an eight-quart Instant Pot, you may need to add ¼ cup water to recipes that do not call for added water.

Customizable

It's very easy to customize many of the dishes by using the beans or grains of your choice. As long as you substitute large beans for each other rather than using cook times for fine split lentils and applying them to giant-size dried lima beans, you should be okay.

Leverage the Science of Pressure Cooking

I am a scientist by training. Not for nothing, but I do have a doctorate in experimental psychology. I am also a gadget geek, as you can see from my various Instant Pot and air-fryer cookbooks. I believe in thoroughly understanding a gadget and how it works and then leveraging that to cook differently.

These recipes skip many of the steps that you use in stovetop or oven cooking, such as browning meat or vegetables. The pressure cooker is capable of browning your food for you (watch my video about the Maillard reaction in a pressure cooker on my blog or YouTube channel). I spent a long time testing and streamlining recipes so that you don't have to. I'll urge you to do what my groups do, which is to #trustUrvashi and try a recipe as written the first time. You can tweak it to your preference the next time around.

Leverage the Power of the Instant Pot

When I buy an Instant Pot cookbook with recipes that require me to sauté on the stovetop, bake in the oven, or fry in an air fryer, then cook in the Instant Pot—all for one dish sometimes—I am driven mad. Very few dishes in this cookbook require this type of "You must surely have elves that wash all hundred pots you just dirtied" type of cooking. Most cook with just the Instant Pot, with some recipes suggesting different ways you can finish them.

Unleash Your Inner Kitchen God or Goddess (or Both)

I see my job as equipping you with the basics you need to cook—and then encouraging you to tweak the recipes so you can make your own adaptations. Trust me when I tell you that inside you, there is a kitchen god or goddess waiting to be unleashed. All he or she needs is a little love and a little knowledge. I am very sure that as you work your way through these recipes, your confidence will grow, your lucky dinner guests will enjoy your cooking, and you'll start to see yourself as an accomplished cook, even if you have never cooked elaborate meals before.

WHY INSTANT POT?

The Instant Pot combines several kitchen appliances in one: pressure cooker, rice cooker, slow cooker, yogurt maker, and sterilizer. Some models can even cook sous vide. But for most people, its most popular function is pressure cooking. A pressure cooker changes the boiling point of water. In the sealed cooking environment, the steam generated by boiling liquid can't escape, so it builds up and creates pressure. As the pressure increases, the boiling point of water is raised. In the Instant Pot, a high pressure of 11.6 psi (pounds per square inch) can raise the boiling temperature of water from 220°F (100°C) to 245°F (118°C). This cooks foods faster and thus retains more flavor. Cooking under pressure infuses food with flavor in a way stovetop cooking can't match.

Speed

The Instant Pot speeds up cooking by two to six times, making it extremely energy efficient while preserving nutrients and resulting in healthy, tasty dishes. This is especially true for tough grains and beans. The Instant Pot is the fastest, easiest, most foolproof way to get these done.

Tough beans like chickpeas and red kidney beans can be prepared in about thirty minutes under pressure and, best of all, require no stirring or watching over the dish as it cooks. Fresh or frozen green peas, sweet corn, and baby carrots can be steamed in two to three minutes. For mashed potatoes, there is no longer a need to boil in water for fifty minutes—instead, steam them for only fifteen minutes.

Hands-Off Cooking

Hands-off cooking is what most people find so appealing about cooking with an Instant Pot. Once you place your food in it and set the appropriate cooking time, you can be assured that the food will cook as it should and you'll be presented with a tasty meal when it's done. What's more, your meal will be kept warm until you're ready to eat.

Better Nutrition and Taste

The fully sealed environment of the Instant Pot traps the flavors, nutrients, and aromas of the food instead of releasing them throughout your home. Heat is distributed evenly, deeply, and quickly once pressure builds up. Minimal water is required for steaming, so vitamins and minerals are not leached or dissolved. Greens retain their bright colors, meats are well cooked, and whole grains and beans are perfectly tender and delicious.

No, It's Not Actually "Instant"

I have tried hard to list reasonable prep and cooking times for the recipes in this book, but the total time for a recipe also includes the time it takes for your pot to come to pressure as well as for the pressure to be released. In this book, we assumed ten minutes for the pot to come to pressure. Total cook time is prep time, plus ten minutes for the pot to come to pressure, plus cooking time under pressure, plus the pressure release time.

The first time you make a recipe, allow thirty to forty-five minutes for the entire process, even if a recipe says it cooks in fifteen minutes under pressure. How long it takes for the pot to come to pressure is controlled by many factors:

- How much food is in the pot: A fuller pot takes longer to come to pressure.
- Whether the food was frozen when you started: While cooking time under pressure will be the same, the time it takes to build pressure will be longer with frozen foods.
- How much liquid you have in the pot: more liquid means it takes longer to

build pressure. This is why some of my recipes ask you to use very little water up front but then say to thin the dish with water after cooking to reach the right consistency.

No Need to Sauté for Browning: One of the most common mistakes people make when cooking with or writing recipes for a pressure cooker is to brown foods excessively before cooking under pressure. I have created a video on twosleevers.com about how the pressure cooker encourages the Maillard reaction without the need to brown foods ahead of time. It's quite nerdy and geeky but hopefully also informative—kinda like me! So stop browning your meats ahead of time, and just let the pressure cooker do the work for you. Stop evaporating the flavorful liquids out of vegetables and then adding plain water to compensate. Just cook like I ask you to and you can save time and effort while leveraging the pressure cooker's abilities.

An Unwatched Pot: Once the pot is sealed, there's no need to watch the beans and test them repeatedly to prevent undercooking or to stir continuously to keep the things from burning. If you're like me and are easily distracted by shiny objects, you'll find the Instant Pot to be a blessing.

Heat Efficiency and Odors: Not leaving your oven on for hours, not heating up your kitchen, and not having smells permeate throughout your house can be a wonderful thing. Not having to turn on your oven to make a cake is a great thing especially during the summer.

Cooking on the Road and in Small Spaces: Many people use their Instant Pots while traveling, while camping in RVs, in boats, in hotel rooms, in smaller apartments, and in dorms where there might not be access to multiple appliances, ovens, or large amounts of counter space. The ability to multitask is a huge advantage of this multicooker.

INSTANT POT TERMS TO KNOW AND WHEN TO USE THEM

PIP (Pot-in-Pot) Cooking

This refers to the practice of cooking multiple dishes at the same time in your pressure cooker. This is accomplished by using the steamer rack and an additional heatproof pot that fits in the inner pot. Typically, one dish is cooked directly in the inner pot, while another dish is cooked in a smaller pot that rests on the steamer rack.

You will place water in the inner liner of the Instant Pot to generate steam. You may also be asked to place water inside the small heatproof pot that holds the ingredients being cooked, such as beans, rice, etc. If you are only steaming vegetables lightly, you may not be required to put water into the heatproof pot.

A simple rule of thumb is that anything that absorbs water while cooking (rice, beans, pasta, potatoes, and other starches) requires added water. Anything that releases water (like most nonstarchy vegetables) doesn't require water to cook but may benefit from broths and sauces to add flavor.

NPR (Natural Pressure Release) and QPR (Quick Pressure Release)

Once the Instant Pot has finished the cook cycle, it will beep to let you know. At this point, most recipes direct you to release pressure naturally, quickly release the pressure, or sometimes to use a combination of the two, such as allowing the pot to release pressure naturally for ten minutes and then quickly releasing the remaining pressure.

NPR: To release pressure naturally, simply allow the pot to rest undisturbed after the cook cycle has finished. As it cools, it will gradually release pressure until the float valve drops, indicating that the pot is no longer under pressure. You do not need to turn off the Keep Warm feature to enable NPR. The pot will drop both temperature and pressure on its own and move to the Keep Warm setting (unless you've expressly disabled it), allowing you to enjoy your dinner when you're ready. The short version is NPR = do nothing and wait patiently for the pin to drop.

QPR: To release pressure quickly, press down on the button on top of the lid or turn the dial on the steam valve to Venting. This allows the pot to release steam and pressure. Ensure that the pot is not directly under cabinets that may be damaged by the hot steam, and be sure to keep your hands and face away from the steam. Do not allow children to "help" with this.

What Are All These Buttons and Do I Really Need Them All?

Even though I have been using my Instant Pot for years, I do understand the bewilderment that accompanies the acquisition of a new Instant Pot. There are so many buttons! Standing in front of your new Instant Pot, you stare at the control panel, wondering if you're about to cook dinner or launch a rocket. The instrument panel has stopped many a hungry person in her tracks, but I'm going to make this very easy for you.

In this book, almost all the recipes use just two settings: Sauté, plus Pressure Cook (for those with the Ultra model) or Manual (for those with the Duo or Lux models). Those are the only settings you need to cook most of these recipes.

Having said that, it's good to understand what the other settings do. (If you're more of a visual learner, I have a video on this topic on my blog.) It's a common misperception that all the settings are really the same, just programmed with different times. Many—but not all—of the buttons are unique in some combination of time, pressure, and temperature. According to my testing, there are six settings that have specific functions rather than just different time programs, as I've detailed below.

Understanding the Six Most Important Buttons on Your Instant Pot

There are sixteen buttons on the Instant Pot (depending on the model), broken down as follows: The pressure-cook programs include: Ultra, Pressure Cook, Meat/Stew, Soup/Broth, Bean/Chili, Steam, Sterilize, Rice, Multigrain, Porridge, Egg, and Cake.

The nonpressure cook programs include: Slow Cook, Sauté, Warm, and Yogurt.

Sauté: This functions exactly like a pan on the stovetop to brown and sear, and you can set it to High, Medium, or Low temperatures. This is not pressure cooking, just heating and browning.

Pressure Cook/Manual: This will likely be your most often used button. The buttons usually default to High pressure, and you can set the cooking time. When a recipe says, "Set to HIGH pressure for 5 minutes," for example, this is the button you'll reach for, and then you'll likely use the +/− buttons (or a dial) to set the cooking time to five minutes.

Soup: When you use the Soup button, the pressure cooker heats up very slowly at first, before hitting higher temperatures. It was originally designed to create noncloudy broths for soups. I find it quite useful when you are trying to keep yogurt or other liquids from separating.

Steam: Confusingly, it's called Steam, but it's under pressure. When you use this button, the pot raises its temperature very quickly—and it stays hot. This allows your food to cook very quickly without a longer lead time before the pot comes to pressure. This is very useful when you're cooking delicate items such as vegetables. You must, however, use a steamer rack if you use the Steam function. Do not place food directly on the bottom of the pot or it will likely scorch.

Yogurt: Making yogurt at home ensures that you know exactly what went into it and allows you to customize it to better suit your family's tastes. I also use this function to sprout beans and to proof bread dough. One caveat, though: Do not use the Instant Pot lid when proofing dough. Use a glass lid or other easily removable lid. If your bread rises a little too enthusiastically, you may find the lid stuck tight with no easy way to remove it.

Slow Cook: There are many debates as to whether an Instant Pot can slow cook well. My experience suggests that it can—with a caveat. Forget everything you know about settings on a slow cooker, because the Instant Pot has settings of its own:

- Low on an Instant Pot = Warm on a regular slow cooker
- Medium on an Instant Pot = Low on a regular slow cooker
- High on an Instant Pot = High on a regular slow cooker

If this is confusing, just remember this: Don't use the Low setting to cook. Use either Medium or High, and you'll be fine. I suggest you try your first slow-cooked recipe on a day you'll be at home rather than at the end of a long day at work, so you're not adding confusion and frustration to hunger.

You can leave the steam vent open or closed when you slow cook.

Pressure Cooking at High Altitudes

The higher the altitude, the lower the atmospheric pressure. In cooking, this means that the higher the altitude, the lower the boiling point of water (and other liquids), and the faster the water evaporates. When you get above an altitude of 2,000 feet above sea level, this can be significant. While the sealed interior of a pressure cooker helps make up for the lower atmospheric pressure, you'll still have to make some adjustments if you live in the mountains and if you have any model of the Instant Pot other than the Ultra.

Most pressure cooker manufacturers recommend increasing cooking times by 5 percent for every 1,000 feet above 2,000 feet, so a dish that cooks under pressure for 20 minutes at sea level would cook for 21 minutes at 3,000 feet or 22 minutes at 4,000 feet. Some manufacturers also recommend increasing the amount of liquid slightly.

If you have the Instant Pot Ultra, there's no need to adjust cooking times. This model allows you to specify your altitude up to 9,900 feet, and the machine will adjust cooking times accordingly.

FREQUENTLY ASKED QUESTIONS

I often post Instant Pot recipes on my blog, twosleevers.com, as well as on my Facebook pages and groups, and I always get lots of comments and feedback, which I love. While many people quickly master a few recipes, many wish to do even more with the appliance. Even though it's my priority to create easy, simple recipes, I still want those recipes to help you explore and enjoy your appliance, as well as expand your palate. Here is a collection of some of the questions I get asked most often and my answers to help you on your journey as you cook with the Instant Pot.

Equipment Questions

My pot is spitting steam.

Note where the steam appears to be coming from. If it's coming from the valve, it's not unusual for the pot to release a little steam as it comes up to pressure; and once the valve floats up and seals, it should stop leaking steam. If, however, you're getting a steady flow of steam from the sealing ring, the seal is not tight or may need replacing. In this case, the pot will not come to pressure. Turn it off, and reset or replace the seal.

My lid won't open.

If your lid won't open, the pot is likely under pressure. Do not force it! Wait for all the pressure to be released before you try again. Forcing it can result in serious burns and injuries. If you've been waiting for twenty-five to thirty minutes and it still won't open, and the float valve is still up, it's possible something is stuck under the valve. Very carefully, using a long-handled spoon or fork, gently tap the float valve. This is usually enough to get the valve to drop. Clean the lid and the valve carefully before you begin the next cooking cycle.

My lid won't close.

If your lid won't close, the most likely culprit is the sealing ring. Remove it and reinsert it following the directions that came with the Instant Pot. Ensure there is no food or debris lodged in the sides of the lid or the rim of the pot. Ensure that the liner you're using is the correct one.

The second most common reason is that you've opened the pot and decided you needed to cook the food a little longer, but now the lid won't go back on easily. The steam in the pot often pushes the valve up in these situations. Turn the float valve to Venting to allow some of that steam to dissipate, and try again.

I've been waiting for forever for the pin to drop, but it says it's still locked.

Hmm . . . "forever" is kinda relative, isn't it? Okay, jokes aside, realize that a very full pot, especially one filled with liquid, takes longer to come to pressure and longer to release pressure. If you're sure you've given it plenty of time on its own, the float valve may be stuck. Very carefully, using a long-handled spoon or fork, gently tap the float valve. This is usually enough to get the valve to drop. Clean the lid and the valve carefully before the next cooking cycle.

My sealing ring smells like the last savory thing I cooked. How do I get rid of the odor?

A few things work to keep the sealing ring from retaining odors:

- Remove and wash it each time, but don't forget to put it back before cooking again!

- Prop the lid on the side of the pot to allow both pot and lid to air out.
- Odd though it may sound, soaking the ring in a sink full of water along with a denture-cleaning tablet is quite effective.
- Wash the ring well and put it out in the sun to dry. This method is highly effective but, of course, quite impractical on a dreary winter day.

General Food Questions

Why is my food under-/overcooked?

The most common reasons for under- or over-cooked food are:

- Insufficient water in the recipe (undercooked)
- Pieces of food were larger (undercooked) or smaller (overcooked) than what the recipe called for
- Doing NPR when the recipe calls for QPR (overcooked), or QPR when the recipe calls for NPR (undercooked)

Why does my food keep burning?

The most common reasons for burning are:

- Insufficient water in the recipe
- Substituting ingredients that absorb water into the recipe (e.g., potatoes, pasta, rice, grains, beans, and legumes) for ingredients that release water (e.g., most meats and vegetables)

- Food stuck to the bottom of the pot while sautéing (I cannot overemphasize the necessity of deglazing thoroughly in an Instant Pot.)
- Thick liquids, such as tomato sauces, thick cream soups, etc., being used to bring the pot to pressure. If you must use these thick liquids, use plain water at the bottom, then the meat or vegetables, and layer the thick liquids on top without stirring.
- Inadequate seal causing water to evaporate

I thought we had to have 1 cup of water for the Instant Pot to come to pressure. How is it that your recipes often have no added water?

You do need water for the Instant Pot to come to pressure, but I prefer to get that water directly from the meat and vegetables rather than adding tap water. Most meats and vegetables release a lot of water as they cook. This flavorful broth seasons the dish better than tap water. It also keeps you from having to boil away the excess water at the end, which can result in an overcooked dish. Pressure cooking imparts a better taste because it keeps your meal from being boiled as it cooks. Using the Sauté function to boil off excess water defeats that purpose.

Note, however, that rice, beans, lentils, and other legumes do require water to cook. They absorb water and swell (and foam) as they cook, but they require a lot less water than stovetop cooking. This is largely because, on a stovetop, you lose most of the water through evaporation. In a contained and sealed environment, water loss is kept to a minimum. Use the water amounts specified in these recipes and in pressure-cooking charts for best results.

I used my Slow Cook function, but hours later my food is still raw. Why?

Your Instant Pot is a fully functional slow cooker that is capable of producing delicious slow-cooked meals. If you have been using a traditional slow cooker, the following may be helpful for you.

- The Low setting should be used to keep foods warm not to cook foods.
- The Medium setting functions much like the Low setting on a traditional slow cooker. Use the Medium setting for slow-cooking meats all day (e.g., making a roast in eight hours).
- The High setting functions much like the High setting on a traditional slow cooker. Use this setting for slightly faster slow cooking (e.g., making a roast in four hours).

Yogurt Questions

I left my yogurt in for longer than eight hours. Is it spoiled?

Yogurt can be left to incubate safely for twelve to fourteen hours. After that, it will not spoil, but it might be tarter than you prefer. The longer it incubates, the tarter it will taste.

I followed all the directions, but my yogurt did not set.

The most common reasons for yogurt not setting are:

- Your yogurt starter may need to be replaced; it may be either old or not contain sufficient live cultures. Get some new starter, add it to the unset batch, and try again.
- The milk temperature was too high when the starter was added and killed the live cultures in the starter. Get some new starter, add it to the unset batch, and try again.

Egg Questions

I followed all the directions, but my eggs are still under- or overcooked or green around the yolks. Why?

Let's just be honest with each other. Eggs are the temperamental fillies of the Instant Pot world. They perform beautifully on a good day, and on other days, they will mess you up. Within the same batch of cooked eggs, the devils with their gray yolks will nestle up innocently beside the angels with their perfect yellow yolks. But with a little experimentation, the pressure cooker can give you perfectly cooked eggs. Since people prefer their eggs at different consistencies, I suggest you experiment to find the time that is best for you.

Recommended cooking times for perfect eggs:

- Soft-boiled: 2 minutes, QPR, ice bath
- Hard-boiled: 5 minutes, 5 minutes NPR, ice bath

Cake Questions

Is the cake really baking in there?

The pressure cooker is not an oven, so the cake is not technically being baked. It is, however, being steamed, resulting in a well-prepared cake.

What is the texture of cakes baked in an Instant Pot?

A cake or quick bread baked in an Instant Pot will be lighter and fluffier than an oven-baked one. Try it for yourself and see how you can make delectable quick breads and cakes without turning on the oven!

Cooking Times

Why does it take so long for the pot to come to pressure?

The amount of time it takes the pot to come to pressure is influenced by:

- The amount of food in the pot. A fuller pot will take longer to come to pressure.

- The type of food in the pot. Liquids take longer to come to pressure than denser foods. Frozen foods will take longer to come to pressure as well.

If I double the ingredients, do I double the cooking time?

No, you keep cooking time the same. It may take the cooker a little longer to come to pressure, but once under pressure, cooking time is the same. You can vary the number of servings for any of these recipes without increasing the cooking time—under pressure, that is. But the fuller your pot, the longer it will take to come to pressure. Once under pressure, however, one cup of beans will cook as quickly as two cups of beans—so allow longer total cooking times, but do not increase the cooking time under pressure.

Since this question is asked so often, let me use an example. Let's say you're making tea and you need to let the tea steep for 5 minutes. If you're making 4 cups of tea, your 4 cups of water will come to a boil very quickly, and you then steep the tea for 5 minutes. If you're making 10 cups of tea, the 10 cups of water will take longer to come to a boil, but you'll still only steep the tea for 5 minutes. It's the same with pressure cooking. When you double a recipe, the time it takes for the pot to come to pressure increases (boiling 4 cups of water versus 10 cups of water), but the time it takes for the item to cook under pressure stays the same (steeping the tea for 5 minutes).

Can I cook food from frozen without first defrosting it?

Many of these recipes call for frozen vegetables. This is done deliberately. I am using this as a way to slow down cooking so that your vegetables do not overcook.

When should I use natural pressure release versus quick pressure release?

Many of the recipes call for a combination of both. I prefer to use natural release for ten minutes and then quick release the remaining pressure. There are two situations where I use quick release only:

- Many vegetables require a short cooking time. Natural pressure release results in an overcooked dish.
- Quick release is often used when you plan to add items to a dish halfway through cooking. This style of cooking in stages can be quite useful in recipes that ask you to cook the beans for a lot longer than the greens. In this case, you release pressure quickly after cooking the beans, add the greens, and then release pressure quickly at the end to avoid overcooking.

LET'S COOK

It's time to start cooking. You know everything you need to know to cook delicious meals in your Instant Pot and to produce food in your own kitchen that will rival what you can get in restaurants. If you can chop, mix, blend, stir, and press buttons, you can make these recipes. None of them call for complicated techniques. Children as young as ten years old have made many of these recipes with success. Children under two years old have eaten these with great enjoyment, as pictures I'm sent of sweet little faces smeared with butternut squash soup often remind me.

Remember that you know your family's tastes better than I do, so if you know they will hate a particular ingredient (hello, cilantro!) or that an ingredient might be too spicy for them (goodbye, cayenne!), change it up to personalize the dish. I am told that I use less salt than many others. Add more or less to suit your tastes.

Finally, keep in mind that when you make these recipes, you'll not only have better-tasting, more authentic, more nutritious food at home, you'll also be saving a lot of money. In just three or four meals, the savings will be enough to justify buying another Instant Pot! If you're looking for a reason to become a two-pot household, now you have it. You're welcome.

Let's use our Instant Pots to explore the varied world of food that awaits us!

VEGETABLES

BEET AND YOGURT SALAD

I grew up eating this salad in India. Think of this as a great base recipe, where you can switch out the beets for other vegetables. I often use lightly steamed carrots instead of the beets. Oh, and once you cook beets in a pressure cooker, you'll never cook them any other way. Fast, easy, and the peel slides right off.

ACTIVE TIME	FUNCTION	RELEASE	TOTAL TIME
15 minutes	Manual (High)	Natural/Quick	1 hour

Egg-Free · Gluten-Free · Grain-Free · Soy-Free · Vegetarian · SERVES 4 as a side dish

1 cup water

4 large beets, trimmed and halved

½ cup Greek yogurt

⅛ cup dry-roasted peanuts, chopped

½ cup chopped fresh cilantro

1 teaspoon kosher salt

2 tablespoons vegetable oil

1 teaspoon cumin seeds

½ teaspoon ground turmeric

PER SERVING

Calories: 250
Total Fat: 19g
Saturated Fat: 5g
Sodium: 580mg
Carbohydrates: 16g
Fiber: 5g
Sugars: 9g
Protein: 8g

1. Pour the water into the Instant Pot. Place a trivet in the pot. Place the beets on the trivet.

2. Secure the lid on the pot. Close the pressure-release valve. Select MANUAL and set the pot at HIGH pressure for 10 minutes. At the end of the cooking time, allow the pot to sit undisturbed for 10 minutes, then release any remaining pressure.

3. Transfer the beets to a bowl of water for 10 minutes and allow to cool. Slip off the peels and dice.

4. In a large bowl, combine the beets, yogurt, peanuts, cilantro, and salt.

5. In a small heatproof pan or tadka ladle, heat the oil. Once the oil is hot, add the cumin seeds. Once the seeds start to sputter and pop, remove them from the heat source. Stir in the turmeric and allow to sizzle for 5 to 10 seconds. Pour the flavored oil over the beets.

6. Mix well. Allow the salad to stand for 15 to 30 minutes at room temperature before serving.

BRAISED GREEN BEANS WITH HAM

If you grew up in the South and have had green beans that have cooked all day, you will appreciate how the Instant Pot can reproduce that flavor in just a few minutes. If you haven't tried them, however, you must make this immediately. Not a "squeaker" in this bunch!

ACTIVE TIME	FUNCTION	RELEASE	TOTAL TIME
10 minutes	Manual (High)	Natural/Quick	35 minutes

Egg-Free • Nut-Free • Dairy-Free • Gluten-Free • Grain-Free • Soy-Free • Low-Carb •
SERVES 6 as a side dish

1 cup diced onion

1 cup diced ham

1 teaspoon kosher salt

1 teaspoon black pepper

¼ cup water

6 cups green beans, halved

PER SERVING

Calories: 70
Total Fat: 2g
Saturated Fat: 0g
Sodium: 620mg
Carbohydrates: 9g
Fiber: 3g
Sugars: 4g
Protein: 6g

1. In the Instant Pot, combine the onion, ham, salt, pepper, and water and mix well. Place the green beans on top.

2. Secure the lid on the pot. Close the pressure-release valve. Select MANUAL and set the pot at HIGH pressure for 4 minutes. At the end of the cooking time, allow the pot to sit undisturbed for 10 minutes, then release any remaining pressure.

BRAISED LEEKS

Never had braised leeks before? Me neither, until I was staring at a large pile of leeks sitting on my kitchen counter, begging to be made into something delicious. The little touch of honey adds a wonderful sweetness to it, but you can always switch it out for a low-carb sweetener if you prefer.

ACTIVE TIME	FUNCTION	RELEASE	TOTAL TIME
10 minutes	Manual (High)	Quick	25 minutes

Egg-Free • Nut-Free • Dairy-Free • Gluten-Free • Grain-Free • Soy-Free • Vegan • Low-Carb • 30 Minutes or Less • SERVES 4 as a side dish

1½ pounds leeks (about 2 large leeks, white and light green parts only)

½ teaspoon kosher salt

¾ cup water

4½ teaspoons melted butter or butter substitute, such as Earth Balance

1 tablespoon fresh lemon juice

1½ teaspoons honey or ½ teaspoon Splenda

½ teaspoon garlic powder

PER SERVING

Calories: 110
Total Fat: 5g
Saturated Fat: 3g
Sodium: 540mg
Carbohydrates: 18g
Fiber: 2g
Sugars: 6g
Protein: 2g

1. Cut the leeks in half lengthwise. Discard the outer leaves and rinse each half well, fanning the layers under the water to get rid of the grit.

2. In the Instant Pot, combine the leeks, salt, and water.

3. Secure the lid on the pot. Close the pressure-release valve. Select MANUAL and set the pot at HIGH pressure for 2 minutes. At the end of the cooking time, use a quick release to depressurize.

4. Using tongs, carefully transfer the leeks to a serving dish.

5. In a small bowl, whisk together the butter, lemon juice, honey, and garlic powder.

6. Pour the sauce over the leeks and serve immediately.

BRAISED LETTUCE WITH PEAS AND CARROTS

This is a super-easy and tasty way to use up that lettuce you bought, absolutely sure that you'd be eating lots of salads that week—only to find it glaring balefully at you a few days later. Braising it with a handful of other ingredients reduces it to a tasty side dish that you will actually eat—unlike that lettuce salad you keep planning on making.

ACTIVE TIME	FUNCTION	RELEASE	TOTAL TIME
5 minutes	Manual (High)	Quick	15 minutes

Egg-Free • Nut-Free • Gluten-Free • Grain-Free • Soy-Free • Vegetarian • Low-Carb • 30 Minutes or Less • SERVES 4 as a side dish

¼ cup water

1 teaspoon kosher salt

1 teaspoon black pepper

4 cups frozen peas and carrots

1 cup diced green onions

3 tablespoons butter, diced

4 cups thickly sliced romaine lettuce

½ cup fresh parsley

2 tablespoons fresh lemon juice

1. In the Instant Pot, combine the water, salt, and pepper. Add the peas and carrots. Sprinkle the green onions over the top. Dot with butter cubes. Scatter the lettuce on top. Do not stir.

2. Secure the lid on the pot. Close the pressure-release valve. Select MANUAL and set the pot at HIGH pressure for 0 minutes. At the end of the cooking time, use a quick release to depressurize.

3. Open the lid, stir in the parsley and lemon juice and serve.

PER SERVING

Calories: 170
Total Fat: 10g
Saturated Fat: 6g
Sodium: 670mg
Carbohydrates: 20g
Fiber: 7g
Sugars: 1g
Protein: 6g

CABBAGE AND POTATO SOUP (SHCHI)

This is a super-simple Russian soup (traditionally called Shchi) and is made from very humble ingredients—but absolutely delicious. I am often lavish with the sour cream in this recipe. It adds a wonderful creaminess to the soup, but you can also enjoy the natural flavors of the vegetables in a clear broth if you prefer.

ACTIVE TIME	FUNCTION	RELEASE	TOTAL TIME
15 minutes	Manual (High)	Natural/Quick	35 minutes

Egg-Free • Nut-Free • Gluten-Free • Grain-Free • Soy-Free • Vegetarian • SERVES 6 as a main dish

2 cups diced celery

2 cups diced red potatoes

1 (14.5-ounce) can diced tomatoes or 1½ cups diced fresh tomatoes

1½ teaspoons kosher salt

1 teaspoon black pepper

2 bay leaves

3 cups water

4 cups chopped cabbage

2 tablespoons apple cider vinegar

¼ cup chopped fresh dill

½ cup sour cream

1. In the Instant Pot, combine the celery, potatoes, tomatoes, salt, pepper, bay leaves, and water. Scatter the cabbage on top. Do not stir.

2. Secure the lid on the pot. Close the pressure-release valve. Select MANUAL and set the pot at HIGH pressure for 3 minutes. At the end of the cooking time, allow the pot to sit undisturbed for 5 minutes, then release any remaining pressure. Discard the bay leaves and stir in the vinegar and dill.

3. Top servings with dollops of sour cream.

PER SERVING

Calories: 100
Total Fat: 4g
Saturated Fat: 2g
Sodium: 690mg
Carbohydrates: 16g
Fiber: 4g
Sugars: 5g
Protein: 3g

CREAMY SPICY GREENS

I find myself creating a lot of recipes out of things that most of us have lying around in the house or pantry. Like you, I often want to make dinner with minimum fuss and without having to make a special shopping trip for a dish. In this case, the coconut milk and lemon juice add a wonderful flavor to the greens, making it a lovely side dish to all kinds of mains.

ACTIVE TIME	FUNCTION	RELEASE	TOTAL TIME
15 minutes	Manual (High)	Natural/Quick	35 minutes

Egg-Free • Nut-Free • Dairy-Free • Gluten-Free • Grain-Free • Soy-Free • Vegan • Low-Carb • SERVES 4 as a side dish

6 cups roughly chopped fresh kale

1 cup diced onion

1 cup diced tomato

¼ cup water

3 cloves garlic, minced

½ to 1 jalapeño pepper, diced

1 tablespoon minced fresh ginger

1 teaspoon kosher salt

1 cup full-fat coconut milk

1 tablespoon fresh lemon juice

PER SERVING

Calories: 150
Total Fat: 12g
Saturated Fat: 11g
Sodium: 500mg
Carbohydrates: 11g
Fiber: 3g
Sugars: 4g
Protein: 3g

1. In the Instant Pot, combine the kale, onion, tomato, water, garlic, jalapeño, ginger, and salt.

2. Secure the lid on the pot. Close the pressure-release valve. Select MANUAL and set the pot at HIGH pressure for 5 minutes. At the end of the cooking time, allow the pot to sit undisturbed for 5 minutes, then release any remaining pressure.

3. Stir in the coconut milk and lemon juice and serve.

CREAMY TOMATO AND CARROT SOUP

I feel very virtuous when I eat this soup—chock-full of nutritious vegetables, yet the puréeing makes it easy to feed it to picky diners who resist vegetables.

ACTIVE TIME	FUNCTION	RELEASE	TOTAL TIME
15 minutes	Manual (High)	Natural/Quick	35 minutes

Egg-Free • Nut-Free • Gluten-Free • Grain-Free • Soy-Free • Vegetarian • Low-Carb •
SERVES 4 as a side dish

2 cups chopped carrots

1 (14.5-ounce) can diced fire-roasted tomatoes or 1½ cups fresh diced tomatoes

1 cup diced onion

1 cup chopped round white potatoes

1 teaspoon kosher salt

1 teaspoon black pepper

¼ teaspoon ground cloves

2 cups low-sodium vegetable broth

1 (5-ounce) can evaporated milk

¼ cup chopped fresh parsley

Croutons (optional)

1. In the Instant Pot, combine the carrots, tomatoes, onion, potatoes, salt, pepper, cloves, and broth.

2. Secure the lid on the pot. Close the pressure-release valve. Select MANUAL and set the pot at HIGH pressure for 5 minutes. At the end of the cooking time, allow the pot to sit undisturbed for 10 minutes, then release any remaining pressure. Add the evaporated milk.

3. Using an immersion blender, purée the soup until smooth.

4. Garnish with parsley and croutons, if desired, and serve.

PER SERVING

Calories: 150
Total Fat: 3g
Saturated Fat: 2g
Sodium: 870mg
Carbohydrates: 26g
Fiber: 5g
Sugars: 13g
Protein: 5g

CURRIED PUMPKIN SOUP

Do yourself two favors: Do NOT use curry powder in this. And make your own garam masala. Your tummy, your palate, and your co-diners will thank you!

ACTIVE TIME	FUNCTION	RELEASE	TOTAL TIME
15 minutes	Manual (High)	Natural/Quick	50 minutes

Egg-Free · Nut-Free · Dairy-Free · Gluten-Free · Grain-Free · Soy-Free · Vegetarian · SERVES 4 as a main dish

4 cups chopped pumpkin

1 cup peeled and cored, chopped apple

3 cloves garlic, minced

1 tablespoon minced fresh ginger

1 teaspoon ground turmeric

1 teaspoon kosher salt

1 teaspoon Garam Masala (page 221)

½ teaspoon cayenne pepper

1½ cups low-sodium chicken broth or water

½ cup full-fat coconut milk or heavy cream

Optional toppings:

Bacon crumbles, feta cheese crumbles, or roasted pumpkin seeds

1. In the Instant Pot, combine the pumpkin, apple, garlic, ginger, turmeric, salt, garam masala, cayenne, and broth.

2. Secure the lid on the pot. Close the pressure-release valve. Select MANUAL and set the pot at HIGH pressure for 10 minutes. At the end of the cooking time, allow the pot to sit undisturbed for 10 minutes, then release any remaining pressure.

3. Using an immersion blender, purée the soup until smooth.

4. Serve with a swirl of coconut milk and optional toppings, if desired.

PER SERVING

Calories: 120
Total Fat: 7g
Saturated Fat: 6g
Sodium: 510mg
Carbohydrates: 14g
Fiber: 2g
Sugars: 6g
Protein: 4g

EDAMAME, CORN, AND COUSCOUS SALAD

This is nothing like an ordinary pasta salad! This is a great base salad that you can change up by simply using a different salad dressing in place of the Greek-inspired dressing I've provided here. You could also cut the couscous in half and add other frozen vegetables to the mix, such as peas and carrots, French-cut green beans, or even cooked beans such as chickpeas or kidney beans. The tricolor pearl couscous provides a nice blend of colors, but you can certainly use white couscous if you prefer.

ACTIVE TIME	FUNCTION	RELEASE	TOTAL TIME
10 minutes	Manual (High)	Quick	25 minutes

Egg-Free • Nut-Free • Vegetarian • 30 Minutes or Less • SERVES 4 as a main dish

For the Dressing

2 tablespoons extra-virgin olive oil

2 tablespoons fresh lemon juice

1 clove garlic, minced

2 teaspoons dried oregano

½ teaspoon kosher salt

1 teaspoon black pepper

For the Salad

1 (16-ounce) bag frozen shelled edamame

2 cups frozen corn

2 cups water

1 cup tricolor pearl couscous

½ teaspoon kosher salt

2 cups diced tomatoes

½ cup feta cheese crumbles

1. **For the Dressing:** In a small bowl, whisk together the olive oil, lemon juice, garlic, oregano, salt, and pepper.

2. **For the Salad:** In the Instant Pot, combine the edamame, corn, water, couscous, and salt.

3. Secure the lid on the pot. Close the pressure-release valve. Select MANUAL and set the pot at HIGH pressure for 1 minute. At the end of the cooking time, use a quick release to depressurize.

4. Drain the vegetables and couscous in a colander. Rinse with cold water to stop the cooking process.

5. In a large mixing bowl, combine the vegetable-couscous mixture, tomatoes, feta cheese, and dressing. Toss to mix, and serve.

PER SERVING

Calories: 490
Total Fat: 18g
Saturated Fat: 5g

Sodium: 790mg
Carbohydrates: 60g
Fiber: 10g

Sugars: 8g
Protein: 23g

NAPA CABBAGE AND TOFU SOUP

Simple, comforting, fast. I like napa cabbage in this, but there's no reason you couldn't use regular cabbage or bok choy. For that matter, there's also no reason why you couldn't include other fast-cooking veggies like carrots, peas, or corn in it if you like. You could even throw in a little leftover rice if that sounds good.

ACTIVE TIME	FUNCTION	RELEASE	TOTAL TIME
15 minutes	Manual (High)	Quick	30 Minutes

Egg-Free • Nut-Free • Dairy-Free • Vegan • Low-Carb • 30 Minutes or Less • Grain-Free •
SERVES 6 as a main dish

1 cup thinly sliced onion

1 tablespoon minced fresh ginger

3 cloves garlic, minced

1 tablespoon soy sauce or coconut aminos

5 cups vegetable broth or low-sodium chicken broth

4 cups roughly chopped napa cabbage

8 ounces extra-firm tofu, chopped

½ cup chopped green onions

½ cup chopped fresh cilantro

2 tablespoons sesame oil

1. In the Instant Pot, combine the onion, ginger, garlic, soy sauce, and broth. Place the cabbage on top. Scatter the tofu on top of the cabbage. Do not stir.

2. Secure the lid on the pot. Close the pressure-release valve. Select MANUAL and set the pot at HIGH pressure for 2 minutes. At the end of the cooking time, use a quick release to depressurize.

3. Stir in the green onions, cilantro, and sesame oil and serve.

PER SERVING

Calories: 110
Total Fat: 6g
Saturated Fat: 1g
Sodium: 960mg
Carbohydrates: 9g
Fiber: 2g
Sugars: 3g
Protein: 5g

SPICED SWEET POTATOES

I love making sweet potatoes in the Instant Pot. They're fast, they're evenly cooked, and they require little to no prep. I've used Chinese five-spice powder here, but you can, of course, use other spices like cinnamon and cloves or even apple pie spice for a change.

ACTIVE TIME	FUNCTION	RELEASE	TOTAL TIME
10 minutes	Manual (High)	Natural/Quick	30 minutes

Egg-Free · Gluten-Free · Grain-Free · Soy-Free · Vegetarian · 30 Minutes or Less · SERVES 4 as a side dish

1½ cups water

2 large sweet potatoes, peeled and cut into ¾-inch cubes

2 tablespoons butter

2 tablespoons maple syrup

½ teaspoon kosher salt

½ teaspoon Chinese five-spice powder

½ cup chopped toasted walnuts

PER SERVING

Calories: 230
Total Fat: 15g
Saturated Fat: 5g
Sodium: 310mg
Carbohydrates: 23g
Fiber: 3g
Sugars: 11g
Protein: 4g

1. Pour the water into the Instant Pot. Place a steamer basket in the pot. Place the sweet potatoes in the basket.

2. Secure the lid on the pot. Close the pressure-release valve. Select MANUAL and set the pot at HIGH pressure for 2 minutes. At the end of the cooking time, allow the pot to sit undisturbed for 5 minutes, then release any remaining pressure. Transfer to a serving dish.

3. While potatoes are cooking, in a small microwave-safe bowl, combine the butter, maple syrup, salt, and five-spice powder. Microwave until the butter has melted; stir to combine. (You can also heat this on the stovetop.) Pour the spiced butter over top of the potatoes and stir gently to coat. Sprinkle with walnuts, and serve.

ROSEMARY GREEN BEANS AND TOMATOES

This is an easy go-to meal that you can probably put together with ingredients already in your pantry. Use either fresh or dried rosemary, or switch in your herb of choice. I find this goes really well with Greek food or simply grilled meats.

ACTIVE TIME	FUNCTION	RELEASE	TOTAL TIME
5 minutes	Manual (High)	Natural/Quick	29 minutes

Egg-Free • Nut-Free • Dairy-Free • Gluten-Free • Grain-Free • Soy-Free • Vegan • Low-Carb • 30 Minutes or Less • SERVES 4 as a side dish

1 pound chopped green beans, fresh or frozen

½ cup chopped onion

2 cloves garlic, minced

1 teaspoon dried rosemary

½ teaspoon kosher salt

1 teaspoon black pepper

¼ cup water

1 (8-ounce) can tomato sauce

1. In the Instant Pot, combine the green beans, onion, garlic, rosemary, salt, pepper, and water. Stir well. Pour in the tomato sauce. Do not stir.

2. Secure the lid on the pot. Close the pressure-release valve. Select MANUAL and set the pot at HIGH pressure for 4 minutes. At the end of the cooking time, allow the pot to sit undisturbed for 5 minutes, then release any remaining pressure.

3. Stir well before serving.

PER SERVING

Calories: 60
Total Fat: 0g
Saturated Fat: 0g
Sodium: 520mg
Carbohydrates: 13g
Fiber: 4g
Sugars: 7g
Protein: 3g

SPICY TOMATO-CHEESE GRITS

This spicy, creamy, and slightly sweet version of cheese grits comes together quickly. To reheat, I place them in a covered bowl in the microwave or in a plastic zip-top bag fastened halfway through, and zap them for a few minutes.

ACTIVE TIME	FUNCTION	RELEASE	TOTAL TIME
5 minutes	Manual (High)	Natural/Quick	25 minutes

Egg-Free · Nut-Free · Gluten-Free · Soy-Free · Vegetarian · 30 Minutes or Less · SERVES 6 as a side dish

1 (10-ounce) can diced tomatoes and green chiles

4 cups water, divided

1 tablespoon butter or vegetable oil

½ teaspoon kosher salt

¾ cup grits (not quick-cooking)

1 cup shredded pepper Jack or soy cheese

PER SERVING

Calories: 170
Total Fat: 8g
Saturated Fat: 5g
Sodium: 480mg
Carbohydrates: 18g
Fiber: 1g
Sugars: 0g
Protein: 6g

1. In the Instant Pot, combine the tomatoes and chiles, 2½ cups of the water, butter, and salt. Whisk in the grits, working out the lumps. Pour the mixture into a 7 × 3-inch round heatproof pan.

2. Pour the remaining 1½ cups water into the pot. Place a trivet in the pot. Set the pan on the trivet.

3. Secure the lid on the pot. Close the pressure-release valve. Select MANUAL and set the pot at HIGH pressure for 5 minutes. At the end of the cooking time, allow the pot to sit undisturbed for 10 minutes, then release any remaining pressure.

4. Stir in the cheese, and serve.

NOTE: This dish goes well with grilled shrimp.

VEGAN CREAMED SPINACH

Using silken tofu is an easy way to get a creamy texture into this simple side dish. You won't be able to taste the tofu, just the creamy spinach-iness of this easy and delicious dish.

ACTIVE TIME	FUNCTION	RELEASE	TOTAL TIME
10 minutes	Manual (High)	Natural/Quick	30 minutes

Egg-Free · Nut-Free · Dairy-Free · Gluten-Free · Grain-Free · Vegan · Low-Carb · 30 Minutes or Less ·
SERVES 4 as a side dish

1 cup thinly sliced onion

1 cup stemmed, seeded, and thinly sliced bell pepper (any color)

½ cup water

1 teaspoon kosher salt, divided

1 teaspoon black pepper

½ teaspoon ground nutmeg

12 ounces frozen spinach

½ cup silken tofu

2 tablespoons fresh lemon juice

PER SERVING
Calories: 60
Total Fat: 2g
Saturated Fat: 0g
Sodium: 550mg
Carbohydrates: 10g
Fiber: 4g
Sugars: 3g
Protein: 5g

1. In the Instant Pot, combine the onion, bell pepper, water, ½ teaspoon of the salt, pepper, and nutmeg. Add the spinach on top. Do not stir.

2. Secure the lid on the pot. Close the pressure-release valve. Select MANUAL and set the pot at HIGH pressure for 1 minute. At the end of the cooking time, allow the pot to sit undisturbed for 5 minutes, then release any remaining pressure.

3. Meanwhile, in a blender, combine the tofu, lemon juice, and the remaining ½ teaspoon salt. Blend until smooth.

4. Pour the sauce over the vegetables and stir until the sauce is heated through.

TOMATO-PESTO SOUP

Thick, hearty, complex—this isn't like a tomato soup out of a can. It's a proper grown-up version of tomato soup. Served with a toasted Brie and spicy capicola sandwich, it makes for an amazing—and amazingly fast—dinner.

ACTIVE TIME	FUNCTION	RELEASE	TOTAL TIME
10 minutes	Manual (High)	Natural/Quick	45 minutes

Egg-Free • Soy-Free • Vegetarian • SERVES 6 as a side dish

2 cups water, low-sodium chicken broth, or vegetable broth

2 (14.5-ounce) cans diced fire-roasted tomatoes

4 large cloves garlic, minced

1 cup chopped onion

1 teaspoon kosher salt

½ teaspoon black pepper

2 cups cubed white bread (about 2 slices)

2 tablespoons prepared pesto

1 tablespoon chopped fresh basil (optional)

½ cup shredded Parmesan cheese (optional)

1. In the Instant Pot, combine the water, tomatoes, garlic, onion, salt, and pepper and stir to mix well. Add the bread cubes and stir to combine.

2. Secure the lid on the pot. Close the pressure-release valve. Select MANUAL and set the pot at HIGH pressure for 10 minutes. At the end of the cooking time, allow the pot to sit undisturbed for 10 minutes, then release any remaining pressure. Add the pesto.

3. Using an immersion blender, blend the soup until rich and thick.

4. Divide soup among six bowls. Top with basil and Parmesan cheese, if desired, and serve.

PER SERVING

Calories: 100
Total Fat: 3g
Saturated Fat: 0g
Sodium: 750mg
Carbohydrates: 16g
Fiber: 2g
Sugars: 6g
Protein: 3g

VEGETABLE AND COUSCOUS MEDLEY

Enjoy this one either hot as a side dish or cold as a topping for a pile of fresh greens. You can substitute Swiss chard for the spinach. If you double this dish, use about 1¾ cups of water.

ACTIVE TIME	FUNCTION	RELEASE	TOTAL TIME
10 minutes	Sauté (Normal); Manual (High)	Natural/Quick	30 minutes

Egg-Free • Nut-Free • Dairy-Free • Soy-Free • Vegan • 30 Minutes or Less • SERVES 6 as a side dish

1 tablespoon vegetable oil

2 cups sliced mushrooms

1 cup sliced onion

3 cloves garlic, minced

1 cup Israeli couscous

1 cup water

1 teaspoon kosher salt

½ teaspoon black pepper

4 cups baby spinach

½ cup shredded Parmesan cheese (optional)

PER SERVING

Calories: 130
Total Fat: 3g
Saturated Fat: 0g
Sodium: 330mg
Carbohydrates: 23g
Fiber: 2g
Sugars: 2g
Protein: 4g

1. Select SAUTÉ/Normal on the Instant Pot. When the pot is hot, pour in the oil. Once the oil is hot, add the mushrooms, onion, and garlic. Cook, until the onion softens, about 2 minutes. Select CANCEL.

2. Add the couscous, water, salt, and pepper. Stir well to combine. Top with the spinach. Do not stir.

3. Secure the lid on the pot. Close the pressure-release valve. Select MANUAL and set the pot at HIGH pressure for 2 minutes. At the end of the cooking time, allow the pot to sit undisturbed for 5 minutes, then release any remaining pressure.

4. Gently stir, being careful not to break the couscous. Stir in the Parmesan cheese, if using, and serve.

WILD RICE AND MUSHROOM SOUP

This soup uses a scant ½ cup of wild rice, but cooks it until it is very tender and almost bursting, which adds a lovely creaminess to the soup. You can always stir cooked rotisserie chicken into the finished soup to make a heartier main dish, or enjoy as-is for a soup course.

ACTIVE TIME	FUNCTION	RELEASE	TOTAL TIME
10 minutes	Manual (High)	Natural/Quick	55 minutes

Egg-Free • Nut-Free • Gluten-Free • Grain-Free • Soy-Free • Vegetarian • SERVES 4 as a main dish

2 cups baby carrots, chopped lengthwise

2 cups sliced mushrooms

1 cup chopped onion

1 cup chopped celery

½ cup wild rice

3 cloves garlic, minced

1½ teaspoons poultry seasoning

1½ teaspoons kosher salt

4 cups water, plus more if needed

1 (5-ounce) can evaporated milk

1. In the Instant Pot, combine the carrots, mushrooms, onion, celery, rice, garlic, poultry seasoning, salt, and water.

2. Secure the lid on the pot. Close the pressure-release valve. Select MANUAL and set the pot at HIGH pressure for 20 minutes. At the end of the cooking time, allow the pot to sit undisturbed for 10 minutes, then release any remaining pressure. Stir in the evaporated milk.

3. Use an immersion blender to purée about half the mixture. Add water, if needed, to achieve desired consistency. Serve hot.

PER SERVING

Calories: 180
Total Fat: 4g
Saturated Fat: 2g
Sodium: 820mg
Carbohydrates: 31g
Fiber: 4g
Sugars: 10g
Protein: 8g

POULTRY AND EGGS

CAJUN-STYLE CHICKEN AND OKRA STEW

This recipe is a good example of why I test recipes so thoroughly. I had originally written it to have cornbread on top. It was . . . interesting. It was actually quite tasty but only pretty enough to serve to very good friends or family. So, while I rewrote this very simple stew without it, you could always prepare a small box of cornbread mix and pour it on top of the chicken, and cook as directed without stirring. The cornbread cooks into a nice dome on top of the stew.

ACTIVE TIME	FUNCTION	RELEASE	TOTAL TIME
10 minutes	Manual (High)	Natural/Quick	40 minutes

Egg-Free · Nut-Free · Dairy-Free · Gluten-Free · Grain-Free · Soy-Free · SERVES 4

1 pound boneless skinless chicken thighs, each cut into 3 pieces

1 (14.5-ounce) can diced tomatoes

1 (10-ounce) package frozen cut okra

1 cup diced onion

½ cup diced celery

½ cup stemmed, seeded, and roughly chopped bell pepper (any color)

1 tablespoon minced fresh ginger

1 to 1½ tablespoons Cajun Spice (page 220)

1 teaspoon dried thyme

1 teaspoon kosher salt

½ cup water

1. In the Instant Pot, combine the chicken, tomatoes, okra, onion, celery, bell pepper, ginger, Cajun Spice, thyme, salt, and water. Stir well.

2. Secure the lid on the pot. Close the pressure-release valve. Select MANUAL and set the pot at HIGH pressure for 10 minutes. At the end of the cooking time, allow the pot to sit undisturbed for 10 minutes, then release any remaining pressure.

3. Serve hot.

PER SERVING

Calories: 210
Total Fat: 5g
Saturated Fat: 2g
Sodium: 850mg
Carbohydrates: 15g
Fiber: 4g
Sugars: 7g
Protein: 25g

CHICKEN AND POTATO CURRY

My husband, Roger, asked me what this curry would be served with, since it already had potatoes. The answer? More carbs! Rice or naan make a great accompaniment for this soup. I usually share and give away my tested recipes, but I kept this one all for myself.

ACTIVE TIME	FUNCTION	RELEASE	TOTAL TIME
15 minutes	Manual (High)	Natural/Quick	35 minutes

Egg-Free · Nut-Free · Dairy-Free · Gluten-Free · Grain-Free · Soy-Free · SERVES 4

1 cup full-fat coconut milk

¾ cup fresh cilantro leaves, divided

5 cloves garlic, peeled

1 serrano pepper, stemmed, seeded if desired

1 (1-inch) piece of ginger, peeled

1 teaspoon kosher salt

1 teaspoon ground turmeric

1 teaspoon Garam Masala (page 221)

½ to 1 teaspoon cayenne pepper

½ cup water

1 pound boneless skinless chicken thighs, cut into bite-size pieces

2 cups chopped long white potatoes

1. In a blender, combine the coconut milk, ¼ cup of the cilantro, garlic, serrano, ginger, salt, turmeric, Garam Masala, and cayenne. Blend until smooth.

2. Pour the coconut sauce into the Instant Pot. Wash out the blender with the water and add to the pot. Stir in the chicken and potatoes.

3. Secure the lid on the pot. Close the pressure-release valve. Select MANUAL and set the pot at HIGH pressure for 4 minutes. At the end of the cooking time, allow the pot to sit undisturbed for 10 minutes, then release any remaining pressure.

4. Sprinkle with the remaining ½ cup cilantro and serve.

PER SERVING

Calories: 310
Total Fat: 17g
Saturated Fat: 12g
Sodium: 600mg
Carbohydrates: 16g
Fiber: 3g
Sugars: 1g
Protein: 25g

CHICKEN AND COUSCOUS SOUP

I had a Syrian employee who invited me for dinner. His wife served this soup as a first course, and I am embarrassed to say I might have had two bowls, leaving me with zero room for dinner. That was eighteen years ago, and I still think about that soup. It occurred to me one day that I could actually make it for myself rather than just dreaming about it, so now we all get to enjoy this lovely, warming, and simple soup.

ACTIVE TIME	FUNCTION	RELEASE	TOTAL TIME
15 minutes	Manual (High)	Natural/Quick	35 minutes

Egg-Free · Nut-Free · Dairy-Free · Soy-Free · SERVES 4

1 pound boneless skinless chicken breasts, each cut into 2 to 3 large chunks

1 cup diced onion

1 cup diced celery

½ cup Israeli couscous

½ cup chopped fresh parsley

3 cloves garlic, minced

1 teaspoon kosher salt

½ teaspoon black pepper

½ teaspoon ground cinnamon

½ teaspoon ground allspice

2½ cups low-sodium chicken broth or water

1. In the Instant Pot, combine the chicken, onion, celery, couscous, parsley, garlic, salt, pepper, cinnamon, allspice, and broth.

2. Secure the lid on the pot. Close the pressure-release valve. Select MANUAL and set the pot at HIGH pressure for 5 minutes. At the end of the cooking time, allow the pot to sit undisturbed for 5 minutes, then release any remaining pressure.

3. Carefully transfer the chicken to a bowl and shred it. Return the chicken to the pot.

4. Stir and serve.

PER SERVING

Calories: 240
Total Fat: 4g
Saturated Fat: 1g
Sodium: 620mg
Carbohydrates: 20g
Fiber: 2g
Sugars: 3g
Protein: 30g

CHICKEN AND VEGETABLE STEW

This simple list of inexpensive ingredients somehow still yields a hearty and healthy chicken soup chock-full of vegetables. All you'll need is good crusty bread with butter or crumbly cheddar for a great meal. The soup reheats well for lunch the next day.

ACTIVE TIME	FUNCTION	RELEASE	TOTAL TIME
20 minutes	Manual (High)	Natural/Quick	40 minutes

Egg-Free · Nut-Free · Dairy-Free · Gluten-Free · Grain-Free · Soy-Free · SERVES 6

1 pound boneless skinless chicken thighs, cut into 2-inch pieces

4 cups chopped cabbage

2 cups chopped long white potatoes

2 cups water or low-sodium chicken broth

1 cup chopped tomato

1 cup diced onion

2 carrots, chopped

¼ cup plus 2 tablespoons chopped fresh cilantro, divided

3 cloves garlic, minced

1 serrano pepper, seeded if desired, chopped

1 tablespoon ground cumin

1½ teaspoons kosher salt

1 teaspoon black pepper

Juice of ½ lemon

1. In the Instant Pot, combine the chicken, cabbage, potatoes, water, tomato, onion, carrots, the ¼ cup cilantro, garlic, serrano, cumin, salt, and pepper.

2. Secure the lid on the pot. Close the pressure-release valve. Select MANUAL and set the pot at HIGH pressure for 3 minutes. At the end of the cooking time, allow the pot to sit undisturbed for 5 minutes, then release any remaining pressure.

3. Open the lid, stir in the lemon juice and the 2 tablespoons cilantro and serve.

PER SERVING

Calories: 170
Total Fat: 4g
Saturated Fat: 1g
Sodium: 580mg
Carbohydrates: 19g
Fiber: 4g
Sugars: 5g
Protein: 18g

CHICKEN POT PIE SOUP

All of the taste of a pot pie filling without the crust. If you would like to use this as filling, however, you can make the recipe with only 1 cup of water and top with a pastry crust. I like to eat most of the broth the first day and then use the thicker leftovers for filling.

ACTIVE TIME	FUNCTION	RELEASE	TOTAL TIME
15 minutes	Manual (High)	Natural/Quick	35 minutes

Egg-Free • Nut-Free • Gluten-Free • Grain-Free • Soy-Free • Low-Carb • SERVES 6

3 cups diced rotisserie chicken

1 cup trimmed green beans

1 cup frozen green peas (optional)

1 cup diced onion

1 cup diced celery

1 cup sliced carrots

2 tablespoons butter

3 cloves garlic, minced

1 teaspoon black pepper

1 teaspoon dried thyme

¼ to ½ teaspoon kosher salt

3 cups low-sodium chicken broth

1 (5-ounce) can evaporated milk

1. In the Instant Pot, combine the chicken, green beans, peas (if using), onion, celery, carrots, butter, garlic, pepper, thyme, salt, and broth.

2. Secure the lid on the pot. Close the pressure-release valve. Select MANUAL and set the pot at HIGH pressure for 2 minutes. At the end of the cooking time, allow the pot to sit undisturbed for 5 minutes, then release any remaining pressure.

3. Open the lid, stir in the evaporated milk, and serve.

NOTE: If you would like to use this as a filling for a pot pie, reduce the broth to 1½ cups. You may also want to thicken with a cornstarch slurry. To make the slurry, in a small bowl, mix 1 tablespoon cornstarch and ¼ cup water. Stir the slurry into the pot after the pressure has been released. Select SAUTÉ/Normal. Cook and stir 3 to 5 minutes or until thickened.

PER SERVING

Calories: 230
Total Fat: 11g
Saturated Fat: 5g
Sodium: 430mg
Carbohydrates: 10g
Fiber: 2g
Sugars: 5g
Protein: 24g

CHICKEN TACO SALAD

The chicken keeps very well, so you could double up on it and use the shredded chicken in a variety of ways all week long.

ACTIVE TIME	FUNCTION	RELEASE	TOTAL TIME
10 minutes	Manual (High)	Natural/Quick	1 hour 10 minutes

Egg-Free • Nut-Free • Dairy-Free • Gluten-Free • Grain-Free • Soy-Free • Low-Carb • SERVES 4

3 tablespoons chili powder

1 tablespoon vegetable oil

1 canned chipotle chile in adobo sauce or 1½ teaspoons ground chipotle pepper

1 teaspoon smoked paprika

1 teaspoon kosher salt

1 teaspoon ground cumin

½ teaspoon cayenne pepper

1 pound boneless skinless chicken breasts, cut into cubes

2 cups sliced onions, divided

¼ cup low-sodium chicken broth

4 cups shredded romaine lettuce

2 cups cherry tomatoes, halved

Optional toppings:
guacamole, crushed tortilla chips, salsa, grated cheddar cheese

1. In a small bowl, combine the chili powder, oil, chipotle chile, paprika, salt, cumin, and cayenne. Whisk until well combined.

2. Place the chicken in a resealable plastic bag, add the marinade, and seal. Massage until the chicken is well coated. Marinate at room temperature for 30 minutes or in the refrigerator for up to 24 hours.

3. In the Instant Pot, combine the chicken and marinade mixture, 1 cup of the onion, and broth.

4. Secure the lid on the pot. Close the pressure-release valve. Select MANUAL and set the pot at HIGH pressure for 5 minutes. At the end of the cooking time, allow the pot to sit undisturbed for 10 minutes, then release any remaining pressure.

5. Using two forks, shred the chicken.

6. Divide the lettuce among four serving plates. Top with chicken, tomatoes, the remaining 1 cup onion, and optional toppings, if desired.

PER SERVING

Calories: 240	Sodium: 760mg	Sugars: 7g
Total Fat: 8g	Carbohydrates: 16g	Protein: 29g
Saturated Fat: 2g	Fiber: 6g	

CHICKEN TACO SOUP

So simple yet so popular. Yet again, another dinner that doesn't call for a long list of ingredients but tastes creamy and well spiced. It's been very popular with my Facebook followers, since kids and adults alike seem to enjoy this easy recipe. You can also make this with rotisserie chicken. In that case, cook under pressure for five minutes to let the vegetables cook down a little, with a ten-minute natural pressure release.

ACTIVE TIME	FUNCTION	RELEASE	TOTAL TIME
5 minutes	Manual (High)	Natural/Quick	35 minutes

Egg-Free · Nut-Free · Soy-Free · Grain-Free · Gluten-Free · SERVES 4

1 pound boneless skinless chicken tenders

1 (12-ounce) package frozen vegetable soup mix

1 cup frozen corn

2 tablespoons taco seasoning

1 teaspoon kosher salt

3 cups water

1 (5-ounce) can evaporated milk or ⅔ cup full-fat coconut milk

Optional toppings:
shredded Mexican cheese blend, sliced avocado, pickled jalapeños, chopped fresh cilantro

1. In the Instant Pot, combine the chicken, vegetable soup mix, corn, taco seasoning, salt, and water.

2. Secure the lid on the pot. Close the pressure-release valve. Select MANUAL and set the pot at HIGH pressure for 10 minutes. At the end of the cooking time, allow the pot to sit undisturbed for 10 minutes, then release any remaining pressure. Stir in the evaporated milk.

3. Serve with optional toppings, if desired.

PER SERVING
Calories: 270
Total Fat: 6g
Saturated Fat: 3g
Sodium: 750mg
Carbohydrates: 22g
Fiber: 3g
Sugars: 8g
Protein: 31g

CREAMY CHICKEN AND RICE

This is as creamy and comforting as those casseroles made with canned cream soup—except this one doesn't use it. I prefer jasmine rice, which is a little sticky and adds to the overall creaminess.

ACTIVE TIME	FUNCTION	RELEASE	TOTAL TIME
10 minutes	Sauté (Normal); Manual (High)	Natural/Quick	35 minutes

Egg-Free • Nut-Free • Gluten-Free • Soy-Free • SERVES 4

1 tablespoon butter

1 cup diced onion

1 cup sliced mushrooms

3 cloves garlic, minced

1 pound boneless skinless chicken thighs, cut into 2-inch pieces

1 cup jasmine rice, rinsed

1½ teaspoons black pepper, plus more to taste

1 teaspoon kosher salt

1 cup low-sodium chicken broth

1 cup frozen peas and carrots

2 cups chopped baby spinach

½ cup shredded sharp cheddar or pepper jack cheese

½ cup chopped fresh parsley

1. Select SAUTÉ/Normal on the Instant Pot. When the pot is hot, add the butter. Once the butter is melted, add the onion, mushrooms, and garlic. Stir to coat and let sizzle for 10 to 15 seconds.

2. Add the chicken, rice, the 1½ teaspoons pepper, salt, and broth. Stir well. Scatter peas and carrots over the chicken. Scatter the spinach on top. Do not stir.

3. Secure the lid on the pot. Close the pressure-release valve. Select MANUAL and set the pot at HIGH pressure for 4 minutes. At the end of the cooking time, allow the pot to sit undisturbed for 10 minutes, then release any remaining pressure.

4. Open the lid, and gently stir in the cheese.

5. Garnish with parsley, season with pepper to taste, and serve.

PER SERVING

Calories: 430
Total Fat: 13g
Saturated Fat: 6g
Sodium: 770mg
Carbohydrates: 45g
Fiber: 3g
Sugars: 2g
Protein: 33g

CREAMY CHICKEN SOUP

This is a great supper for nights when you haven't recently shopped for groceries, but need to get dinner on the table fast. You can use canned coconut milk instead of the evaporated milk if you prefer.

ACTIVE TIME	FUNCTION	RELEASE	TOTAL TIME
5 minutes	Manual (High)	Quick	20 minutes

Egg-Free · Nut-Free · Gluten-Free · Grain-Free · Soy-Free · Low-Carb · 30 Minutes or Less · SERVES 4

1 pound boneless skinless chicken thighs, cut into cubes (see Note)

1 (10-ounce) package frozen mixed vegetables

1 to 2 teaspoons black pepper

1 teaspoon poultry seasoning

1 teaspoon kosher salt

2 cups low-sodium chicken broth

1 (5-ounce) can evaporated milk

1. In the Instant Pot, combine the chicken, vegetables, pepper, poultry seasoning, salt, and broth.

2. Secure the lid on the pot. Close the pressure-release valve. Select MANUAL and set the pot at HIGH pressure for 2 minutes. At the end of the cooking time, use a quick release to depressurize.

3. Open the lid, stir in the evaporated milk, and serve.

NOTE: You can also make this with leftover cooked chicken. In that case, reduce the cook time to 1 minute at HIGH pressure.

PER SERVING

Calories: 260
Total Fat: 8g
Saturated Fat: 3g
Sodium: 780mg
Carbohydrates: 16g
Fiber: 2g
Sugars: 8g
Protein: 29g

GINGERY CHICKEN SOUP WITH BOK CHOY AND SPINACH

Styled after a Filipino *tinola*, this clear broth soup is made hearty by the addition of the greens and chicken. You could stir some leftover rice into this soup for an all-in-one meal.

ACTIVE TIME	FUNCTION	RELEASE	TOTAL TIME
15 minutes	Manual (High)	Natural/Quick	40 minutes

Egg-Free • Nut-Free • Dairy-Free • Gluten-Free • Grain-Free • Soy-Free • Low-Carb • SERVES 4

1 pound boneless skinless chicken thighs, cut into bite-size pieces

1 cup finely diced onion

2 tablespoons minced fresh ginger

3 cloves garlic, minced

1 tablespoon fish sauce

1 teaspoon kosher salt

½ teaspoon black pepper

3 cups low-sodium chicken broth

4 cups coarsely chopped bok choy

4 cups baby spinach

2 tablespoons fresh lime juice

1. In the Instant Pot, combine the chicken, onion, ginger, garlic, fish sauce, salt, pepper, and broth.

2. Secure the lid on the pot. Close the pressure-release valve. Select MANUAL and set the pot at HIGH pressure for 6 minutes. At the end of the cooking time, allow the pot to sit undisturbed for 5 minutes, then release any remaining pressure.

3. Open the lid, and stir in the bok choy and spinach. Cover the pot and allow the bok choy and spinach to wilt in the residual heat, 2 to 3 minutes.

4. Stir in the lime juice and serve.

PER SERVING

Calories: 210
Total Fat: 6g
Saturated Fat: 2g
Sodium: 1,060mg
Carbohydrates: 10g
Fiber: 2g
Sugars: 3g
Protein: 28g

GREEN ONION RICE WITH CORNISH GAME HEN AND EDAMAME

For this recipe, prepare for the gingery, sticky rice to brown a little at the bottom. It won't burn if you follow the directions exactly (mainly turning off the pot as soon as the ginger and garlic are in and deglazing thoroughly), but the additional ten minutes of rest time really help to add a little crispness. I treat this as a good thing, and mix up the brown bits of flavor and enjoy them!

ACTIVE TIME	FUNCTION	RELEASE	TOTAL TIME
10 minutes	Sauté (Normal); Manual (High)	Natural/Quick	40 minutes

Egg-Free · Nut-Free · Dairy-Free · Gluten-Free · SERVES 4

1 tablespoon toasted sesame oil

1 tablespoon minced fresh ginger

3 cloves garlic, minced

1 cup basmati rice, rinsed

¾ cup chopped green onions, divided

Kosher salt

1 teaspoon black pepper

1¼ cups water

1 cup frozen shelled edamame

1 Cornish game hen, quartered

PER SERVING

Calories: 350
Total Fat: 12g
Saturated Fat: 2g
Sodium: 530mg
Carbohydrates: 40g
Fiber: 4g
Sugars: 1g
Protein: 21g

1. Select SAUTÉ/Normal on the Instant Pot. When the pot is hot, add the sesame oil. Once the oil is hot, add the ginger and garlic and let sizzle, about 10 seconds. Select CANCEL.

2. Add the rice, ½ cup of the green onions, 1 teaspoon salt, pepper, and water. Stir well to ensure nothing is sticking to the bottom of the pot. Scatter the edamame on top of the rice. Do not stir. Season the Cornish game hen inside and out with salt to taste. Place hen quarters on top of the rice. Do not stir.

3. Secure the lid on the pot. Close the pressure-release valve. Select MANUAL and set the pot at HIGH pressure for 4 minutes. At the end of the cooking time, allow the pot to sit undisturbed for 10 minutes, then release any remaining pressure.

4. Remove the hen from the pot and let cool for 5 to 10 minutes. Remove and discard the skin. Remove the meat from the bones and shred. Mix the meat into the rice along with the remaining ¼ cup green onions, and serve.

NOTE: You can also serve the hen quarters without shredding, which is particularly useful if you'd like to separate the dark meat from the white meat when serving your diners. You can also use precooked, shredded chicken in this dish without changing cooking times, but your rice will be a little less flavorful.

JERK CHICKEN AND QUINOA

This is a good recipe to show people that not everything that comes out of an Instant Pot needs to be a soup or stew. While this is a jerk chicken recipe, there's no reason you can't season it in a variety of different ways to keep things interesting.

ACTIVE TIME	FUNCTION	RELEASE	TOTAL TIME
10 minutes	Manual (High)	Natural/Quick	1 hour 10 minutes

Egg-Free • Nut-Free • Dairy-Free • Gluten-Free • Soy-Free • SERVES 4

For the Chicken

2 tablespoons vegetable oil

1 teaspoon sugar

1 teaspoon ground allspice

1 teaspoon ground thyme

1 teaspoon ground oregano

1 teaspoon kosher salt

½ teaspoon ground cinnamon

½ teaspoon cayenne pepper

½ teaspoon garlic powder

1 pound boneless skinless chicken thighs, each cut into 3 pieces

For the Quinoa

1 cup quinoa, rinsed and drained

1 teaspoon kosher salt

2½ cups water, divided

PER SERVING

Calories: 380	Carbohydrates: 30g
Total Fat: 15g	Fiber: 11g
Saturated Fat: 2g	Sugars: 3g
Sodium: 1,080mg	Protein: 29g

1. **For the Chicken:** In a small bowl, combine the oil, sugar, allspice, thyme, oregano, salt, cinnamon, cayenne, and garlic powder. Whisk until well combined.

2. Place the chicken in a resealable plastic bag. Add the marinade, seal, and massage until the chicken is well coated. Marinate at room temperature for 30 minutes or in the refrigerator for up to 8 hours.

3. **For the Quinoa:** In a 6 × 3-inch round heatproof pan, combine the quinoa, salt, and 1 cup of the water. Cover with foil.

4. Pour the remaining 1½ cups water into the Instant Pot. Place a trivet in the pot. Set the pan on the trivet, and place the chicken on top of the foil-covered pan.

5. Secure the lid on the pot. Close the pressure-release valve. Select MANUAL and set the pot at HIGH pressure for 6 minutes. At the end of the cooking time, allow the pot to sit undisturbed for 10 minutes, then release any remaining pressure.

6. Transfer the chicken to a plate. Carefully remove the pan of quinoa from the pot.

7. Serve the chicken over the quinoa.

NOTE: You may choose to brown the chicken slightly before serving.

LEMONY CHICKEN AND RICE SOUP

Inspired by a good old-fashioned Greek *avgolemono*, a lemony chicken and rice soup with beaten eggs stirred in at the end. It has a light touch of lemon to make your soup just a little less run-of-the-mill. I love stirring in the eggs at the end to get cute little egg ribbons.

ACTIVE TIME	FUNCTION	RELEASE	TOTAL TIME
5 minutes	Manual (High); Sauté (Normal)	Natural/Quick	35 minutes

Egg-Free · Nut-Free · Dairy-Free · Gluten-Free · Soy-Free · SERVES 4

1 pound boneless skinless chicken breast, diced

¼ cup Arborio rice, rinsed and drained

1 teaspoon kosher salt

1 teaspoon black pepper

2 cups low-sodium chicken broth

2 tablespoons fresh lemon juice

4 large eggs, beaten (optional)

PER SERVING

Calories: 200
Total Fat: 4g
Saturated Fat: 1g
Sodium: 570mg
Carbohydrates: 11g
Fiber: 1g
Sugars: 0g
Protein: 29g

1. In the Instant Pot, combine the chicken, rice, salt, pepper, and broth. Stir well.

2. Secure the lid on the pot. Close the pressure-release valve. Select MANUAL and set the pot at HIGH pressure for 10 minutes. At the end of the cooking time, allow the pot to sit undisturbed for 10 minutes, then release any remaining pressure.

3. If you are not adding the eggs, stir in the lemon juice and serve. If you are adding the eggs, select SAUTÉ/Normal. When the soup is boiling, slowly pour in the eggs, whisking constantly. Stir in the lemon juice, and serve.

MEXICAN CHICKEN AND RICE SOUP

Everyone should try a *caldo de pollo* at least once, mainly because it may well start a new obsession for you. Chicken, rice, and cumin is such a wonderful combination, and this one tastes like comfort in a bowl.

ACTIVE TIME	FUNCTION	RELEASE	TOTAL TIME
15 minutes	Manual (High)	Natural/Quick	45 minutes

Egg-Free • Nut-Free • Dairy-Free • Gluten-Free • Soy-Free • SERVES 4

1 pound boneless skinless chicken breasts, each cut into 2 to 3 pieces

1 cup canned diced fire-roasted tomatoes

1 cup chopped celery

1 cup chopped carrots

½ cup jasmine rice, rinsed and drained

½ cup chopped onion

5 to 6 sprigs cilantro, with stems

3 cloves garlic, minced

1 teaspoon ground cumin

1 teaspoon kosher salt

4 cups low-sodium chicken broth

1 small avocado, diced (optional)

1. In the Instant Pot, combine the chicken, tomatoes, celery, carrots, rice, onion, cilantro, garlic, cumin, salt, and broth.

2. Secure the lid on the pot. Close the pressure-release valve. Select MANUAL and set the pot at HIGH pressure for 10 minutes. At the end of the cooking time, allow the pot to sit undisturbed for 10 minutes, then release any remaining pressure.

3. Transfer the chicken to a bowl and shred it. Return the chicken to the pot. Remove and discard the cilantro stems.

4. Just before serving, stir in the avocado, if desired.

PER SERVING

Calories: 280
Total Fat: 4g
Saturated Fat: 1g
Sodium: 830mg
Carbohydrates: 28g
Fiber: 2g
Sugars: 5g
Protein: 31g

PEANUT BUTTER CHICKEN

I love the creamy, peanutty flavor that just a dab of peanut butter can add to a dish. I've yet to meet a kid who doesn't like peanut butter, so this ends up being family-friendly as well. If you have a peanut allergy, I'm sure this will work well with nut or seed butters too.

ACTIVE TIME	FUNCTION	RELEASE	TOTAL TIME
10 minutes	Manual (High)	Natural/Quick	35 minutes

Egg-Free • Dairy-Free • Low-Carb • SERVES 4

1 small yellow onion, sliced

3 cloves garlic, minced

1 tablespoon Sichuan peppercorns, roughly crushed

1 tablespoon soy sauce

1 teaspoon red pepper flakes

2 teaspoons sugar or 1 packet Splenda

1 teaspoon kosher salt

½ cup water

1 pound boneless skinless chicken thighs, cut into bite-size pieces

3 tablespoons peanut butter

4 cups coarsely chopped bok choy

Hot cooked rice or shirataki noodles, for serving (optional)

1. In the Instant Pot, combine the onion, garlic, peppercorns, soy sauce, red pepper flakes, sugar, salt, and water. Stir well. Add the chicken.

2. Add dollops of the peanut butter on top. Do not stir. Secure the lid on the pot. Close the pressure-release valve. Select MANUAL and set the pot at HIGH pressure for 5 minutes. At the end of the cooking time, allow the pot to sit undisturbed for 5 minutes, then release any remaining pressure.

3. Open the lid, stir, and scatter the bok choy on top. Cover the pot, and allow the bok choy to cook in the residual heat, about 5 minutes. Stir to combine.

4. Serve over rice or shirataki noodles, if desired.

PER SERVING

Calories: 240
Total Fat: 11g
Saturated Fat: 3g
Sodium: 990mg
Carbohydrates: 8g
Fiber: 2g
Sugars: 5g
Protein: 27g

SAVORY BREAD PUDDING

This is a great make-ahead dish: You can assemble this the night before and cook when ready. You can also freeze the assembled-but-uncooked casserole. Be sure to grease the pan thoroughly so that you can ease out slices.

ACTIVE TIME	FUNCTION	RELEASE	TOTAL TIME
10 minutes	Manual (High)	Natural/Quick	1 hour 10 minutes

Nut-Free · Soy-Free · SERVES 4

Vegetable oil

6 large eggs

1 cup whole milk

½ teaspoon kosher salt

1 teaspoon black pepper

Hot sauce

6 ounces diced low-sodium ham or Canadian bacon

4 slices sourdough bread, cubed

1 cup shredded cheddar cheese

1½ cups water

PER SERVING

Calories: 490
Total Fat: 23g
Saturated Fat: 10g
Sodium: 1,350mg
Carbohydrates: 38g
Fiber: 1g
Sugars: 6g
Protein: 34g

1. Grease a 6-cup Bundt pan with the oil.

2. In a large bowl, whisk together the eggs, milk, salt, pepper, and hot sauce to taste. Stir in the ham, bread, and cheese.

3. Transfer the mixture to the prepared pan and cover with foil.

4. Pour the water into the Instant Pot. Place a trivet in the pot. Set the pan on the trivet.

5. Secure the lid on the pot. Close the pressure-release valve. Select MANUAL and set the pot at HIGH pressure for 40 minutes. At the end of the cooking time, allow the pot to sit undisturbed for 10 minutes, then release any remaining pressure.

WONTON-STYLE MEATBALL SOUP

What's wonderful about this light but filling soup is that you use many of the same ingredients in the meatballs as you do in the soup, which makes it quite efficient. So the long list of ingredients is actually many of the same ingredients but used in two ways. I find it most effective to prep the soup and the meatballs at the same time so I'm only touching each ingredient once.

ACTIVE TIME	FUNCTION	RELEASE	TOTAL TIME
25 minutes	Manual (High)	Natural/Quick	45 minutes

Nut-Free • Dairy-Free • Low-Carb • SERVES 4

For the Soup

4 cups chopped bok choy

1 cup sliced green onions (white and green parts)

½ cup chopped fresh cilantro

1 tablespoon soy sauce

6 cups low-sodium chicken broth

For the Meatballs

1 pound ground chicken or turkey

¼ cup chopped green onions (white and green parts)

¼ cup chopped fresh cilantro or parsley

1 large egg, lightly beaten

1 tablespoon minced fresh ginger

3 cloves garlic, minced

2 teaspoons soy sauce

1 teaspoon black pepper

¼ teaspoon kosher salt

1 to 2 tablespoons toasted sesame oil

1. For the Soup: In the Instant Pot, combine the bok choy, green onions, cilantro, soy sauce, and broth. Stir well.

2. For the Meatballs: In a large bowl, combine the ground chicken, green onions, cilantro, egg, ginger, garlic, soy sauce, pepper, and salt. Mix gently. Using your hands or a small scoop, shape the mixture into meatballs. Place the meatballs in the pot.

3. Secure the lid on the pot. Close the pressure-release valve. Select MANUAL and set the pot at HIGH pressure for 2 minutes. At the end of the cooking time, allow the pot to sit undisturbed for 5 minutes, then release any remaining pressure.

4. Stir in the sesame oil and serve.

EVEN FASTER TIP: Make a double batch of the meatballs. Freeze one half uncooked, or bake and then freeze so you can make the soup even faster next time.

PER SERVING

Calories: 300	Sodium: 880mg	Sugars: 2g
Total Fat: 16g	Carbohydrates: 10g	Protein: 31g
Saturated Fat: 4g	Fiber: 2g	

TURKEY AND KALE SOUP

While I've used cooked turkey for this, you can, of course, use chicken or even frozen meatballs. If you want to start from raw turkey or chicken, just cut up the meat into 4-inch chunks and cook for 8 minutes under pressure. You can then remove the meat, shred it, and put it back into the soup.

ACTIVE TIME	FUNCTION	RELEASE	TOTAL TIME
5 minutes	Manual (High)	Natural/Quick	30 minutes

Egg-Free • Nut-Free • Dairy-Free • Gluten-Free • Grain-Free • Soy-Free • Low-Carb • 30 Minutes or Less • SERVES 4

2 cups diced cooked turkey breast (see Note)

1 (12-ounce) package chopped frozen kale

1 cup chopped onion

2 cloves garlic, minced

1 teaspoon kosher salt

1 teaspoon black pepper

½ teaspoon ground cinnamon

⅛ teaspoon ground cloves

4 cups low-sodium chicken broth

1. In the Instant Pot, combine the turkey, kale, onion, garlic, salt, pepper, cinnamon, cloves, and broth.

2. Secure the lid on the pot. Close the pressure-release valve. Select MANUAL and set the pot at HIGH pressure for 5 minutes. At the end of the cooking time, allow the pot to sit undisturbed for 10 minutes, then release any remaining pressure.

3. Before serving, taste and adjust seasonings as desired.

NOTE: This can be made with uncooked turkey breast as well. If you are using raw turkey, dice it into smaller cubes and cook for 8 minutes on high pressure.

PER SERVING

Calories: 240
Total Fat: 4g
Saturated Fat: 1g
Sodium: 690mg
Carbohydrates: 10g
Fiber: 3g
Sugars: 2g
Protein: 39g

BEEF, PORK, AND LAMB

BEEF AND LEEK STEW

I know that you're told not to cook with cornstarch or flour in an Instant Pot for fear of getting the BURN error. But here's the thing: It will only stick if you don't have enough liquid in the pot to start with. In this recipe, there are two cups of broth, plus all the meat and vegetables release a lot of water. So really there's no reason you can't add the cornstarch at the beginning.

ACTIVE TIME	FUNCTION	RELEASE	TOTAL TIME
15 minutes	Manual (High)	Natural/Quick	40 minutes

Egg-Free • Nut-Free • Dairy-Free • Gluten-Free • Soy-Free • SERVES 4

2 cups dark beer or low-sodium beef broth

2 tablespoons cornstarch

2 tablespoons tomato paste

2 teaspoons dried thyme

1 teaspoon kosher salt

1 teaspoon black pepper

1 pound beef sirloin, cubed

2 cups chopped leeks (white and light green parts)

2 cups chopped carrots

2 bay leaves

½ cup chopped fresh parsley

1. In the Instant Pot, combine the beer, cornstarch, tomato paste, thyme, salt, and pepper. Whisk well. Add the beef, leeks, carrots, and bay leaves.

2. Secure the lid on the pot. Close the pressure-release valve. Select MANUAL and set the pot at HIGH pressure for 10 minutes. At the end of the cooking time, allow the pot to sit undisturbed for 5 minutes, then release any remaining pressure.

3. Discard the bay leaves, stir in the parsley, and serve.

PER SERVING

Calories: 270
Total Fat: 5g
Saturated Fat: 2g
Sodium: 610mg
Carbohydrates: 21g
Fiber: 3g
Sugars: 5g
Protein: 27g

BEEF, BARLEY, AND RICE SOUP

This is not the traditional beef and barley stew that most Americans are used to eating—this one has a few different warm spices in it. The trick here is to cut the meat into bite-size pieces so that it cooks just right in the same time as the barley and rice. Since chuck roasts tend to come in large sizes, I've created quite a few recipes that use chuck roast, including Spicy Beef Barbacoa (page 123) and Rendang-Style Beef and Potatoes (page 116). This way, you can buy one roast and make a variety of different dishes from it.

ACTIVE TIME	FUNCTION	RELEASE	TOTAL TIME
10 minutes	Manual (High)	Natural/Quick	45 minutes

Egg-Free · Nut-Free · Dairy-Free · Soy-Free · SERVES 6

1 pound beef chuck roast, cut into bite-size pieces

3 cups water

1 (14.5-ounce) can fire-roasted tomatoes

1 cup chopped onion

⅓ cup pearled barley (not instant barley)

⅓ cup Arborio rice or jasmine rice

1½ teaspoons kosher salt

1 teaspoon black pepper

¼ teaspoon ground allspice

¼ teaspoon ground cumin

¼ teaspoon ground nutmeg

¼ cup chopped fresh parsley for garnish (optional)

1. In the Instant Pot, combine the meat, water, tomatoes, onion, barley, rice, salt, pepper, allspice, cumin, and nutmeg. Stir well.

2. Secure the lid on the pot. Close the pressure-release valve. Select MANUAL and set the pot at HIGH pressure for 15 minutes. At the end of the cooking time, allow the pot to sit undisturbed for 10 minutes, then release any remaining pressure.

3. Garnish with parsley, if using, and serve.

NOTE: You can also use stew meat rather than chuck roast. This soup would also work with diced boneless skinless chicken thighs instead of beef. In that case, cook for 10 minutes and allow the pot to rest undisturbed for 10 minutes before releasing the remaining pressure.

PER SERVING

Calories: 190	Sodium: 660mg	Sugars: 3g
Total Fat: 3g	Carbohydrates: 23g	Protein: 17g
Saturated Fat: 1g	Fiber: 3g	

BEEF DAUBE

Now here's a stew that's fit for company. A simple salad, a loaf of crusty bread, and you are all set. If you'd like to add wine to this for flavor, you can add in about ¼ cup at the end and boil it down for a few minutes on SAUTÉ. This also reheats well, so it's a great make-ahead.

ACTIVE TIME	FUNCTION	RELEASE	TOTAL TIME
15 minutes	Sauté (Normal); Manual (High)	Natural/Quick	55 minutes

Egg-Free • Nut-Free • Gluten-Free • Soy-Free • SERVES 4

3 tablespoons butter

1 onion, chopped

3 cloves garlic, minced

1 tablespoon tomato paste

1 cup canned diced tomatoes

1 pound beef stew meat

1 to 2 teaspoons kosher salt

1 teaspoon herbes de Provence

½ teaspoon black pepper

1½ cups water, divided

2 cups baby potatoes or chopped turnips

1¾ cups small button mushrooms

2 large carrots, chopped, or 1 cup baby carrots

2 tablespoons cornstarch or 4 teaspoons arrowroot powder

1. Select SAUTÉ/Normal on the Instant Pot. When the pot is hot, add the butter. Once the butter is melted, add the onion, garlic, and tomato paste. Cook, stirring frequently, until the tomato paste is roasted, about 5 minutes.

2. Add the tomatoes, using the liquid from the tomatoes to deglaze the pot, scraping up the browned bits. Add the beef, salt, herbes de Provence, pepper, and 1 cup of the water. Stir well. Layer the potatoes, mushrooms, and carrots on top of the meat.

3. Secure the lid on the pot. Close the pressure-release valve. Select MANUAL and set the pot at HIGH pressure for 5 minutes. At the end of the cooking time, allow the pot to sit undisturbed for 10 minutes, then release any remaining pressure.

4. Select SAUTÉ/Normal on the pot. In a small bowl, mix the cornstarch and the remaining ½ cup water to make a slurry. Stir the slurry into the stew and allow to bubble. Cook, stirring frequently, until thickened, 3 to 5 minutes.

PER SERVING

Calories: 370	Sodium: 790mg	Sugars: 7g
Total Fat: 17g	Carbohydrates: 30g	Protein: 26g
Saturated Fat: 8g	Fiber: 4g	

BEEF STROGANOFF

This is the simplest of recipes but a well-loved one that is perfect for a fast weeknight dinner. If you want to make this with chicken, cook for about 8 to 10 minutes for thighs and about 6 to 7 minutes for chicken breast. I also have a vegetarian version in my *Instant Pot Miracle Vegetarian Cookbook*, as well as on my blog, where you cook the pasta and the mushrooms all in one go.

ACTIVE TIME	FUNCTION	RELEASE	TOTAL TIME
15 minutes	Sauté (High); Manual (High)	Natural/Quick	55 minutes

Egg-Free • Nut-Free • Soy-Free • Low-Carb • SERVES 4

1 tablespoon vegetable oil

1 cup chopped onion

3 cloves garlic, minced

1 pound beef stew meat, cubed

1½ cups chopped mushrooms

1 tablespoon Worcestershire sauce

1 teaspoon kosher salt

½ to 1 teaspoon black pepper

½ cup water

½ cup sour cream

Cauliflower rice, low-carb noodles, or buttered egg noodles for serving (optional)

1. Select SAUTÉ/High on the Instant Pot. When the pot is hot, add the oil. Once the oil is hot, add the onion and garlic. Cook, stirring frequently, 1 to 2 minutes.

2. Add the stew meat, mushrooms, Worcestershire sauce, salt, pepper, and water.

3. Secure the lid on the pot. Close the pressure-release valve. Select MANUAL and set the pot at HIGH pressure for 20 minutes. At the end of the cooking time, allow the pot to sit undisturbed for 10 minutes, then release any remaining pressure.

4. Select SAUTÉ/Normal on the pot. Stir in the sour cream.

5. Serve with cauliflower rice, low-carb noodles, or buttered egg noodles, if desired.

PER SERVING

Calories: 270
Total Fat: 16g
Saturated Fat: 6g
Sodium: 580mg
Carbohydrates: 7g
Fiber: 1g
Sugars: 3g
Protein: 24g

BEEF TERIYAKI AND RICE

Too often, store-bought or restaurant teriyaki sauces are nothing but sugar with a little soy sauce thrown in for funsies. This version is a lot less sweet than what you're probably used to, but the other savory flavors shine through. For a lower-carb option, use frozen riced cauliflower in the pan rather than rice, and use xanthan gum for thickening rather than the cornstarch.

ACTIVE TIME	FUNCTION	RELEASE	TOTAL TIME
20 minutes	Manual (High); Sauté (Normal)	Natural/Quick	35 minutes

Egg-Free • Nut-Free • Dairy-Free • Low-Carb • SERVES 4

For the Beef

1 pound flank steak, cut into strips

1 cup sliced onion

2 tablespoons reduced-sodium soy sauce

2 tablespoons mirin

2 tablespoons water

1 tablespoon sugar or 1 teaspoon Splenda

1 tablespoon grated fresh ginger

½ teaspoon kosher salt

1 teaspoon black pepper

For the Rice

1 cup jasmine rice, rinsed and drained

1 cup water

1 tablespoon vegetable oil

½ teaspoon kosher salt

1. **For the Beef:** In the Instant Pot, combine the steak, onion, soy sauce, mirin, water, sugar, ginger, salt, and pepper. Stir well.

2. **For the Rice:** In a 6 × 3-inch round heatproof pan, combine the rice, water, oil, and salt. Stir well.

3. Place a trivet in the pot. Set the pan on the trivet.

4. Secure the lid on the pot. Close the pressure-release valve. Select MANUAL and set the pot at HIGH pressure for 5 minutes. At the end of the cooking time, allow the pot to sit undisturbed for 10 minutes, then release any remaining pressure.

5. Open the lid, and remove the rice.

recipe continues

For Finishing

1 cup thinly sliced white or yellow onion

1 cup stemmed, seeded, and sliced green bell pepper

¼ cup water

1 tablespoon cornstarch or ¼ teaspoon xanthan gum (see Note)

½ cup sliced green onions

¼ cup sesame seeds

PER SERVING

Calories: 480
Total Fat: 15g
Saturated Fat: 4g
Sodium: 770mg
Carbohydrates: 53g
Fiber: 2g
Sugars: 10g
Protein: 31g

6. For Finishing: Select SAUTÉ/Normal on the pot. Add the onion and bell pepper. In a small bowl, mix the water and cornstarch to make a slurry. Stir the slurry into the pot and allow to bubble. Cook, stirring frequently, until thickened, 1 to 2 minutes.

7. Serve over rice. Sprinkle servings with green onions and sesame seeds.

NOTE: If using xanthan gum, sprinkle the gum into the mixture and stir until the sauce thickens.

HAM AND RICE WITH VEGETABLES

This has a lot of the same flavors as fried rice, but they are all cooked together for a fast supper. Since you've got meat, veg, and grains, add a fried egg on top of each serving, and you'll be good to go.

ACTIVE TIME	FUNCTION	RELEASE	TOTAL TIME
10 minutes	Manual (High)	Natural/Quick	35 minutes

Egg-Free • Nut-Free • Dairy-Free • SERVES 4

2 cups diced low-sodium ham

1 cup basmati rice, rinsed and drained

1 cup diced onion

1 cup stemmed, seeded, and roughly chopped green, yellow, or orange bell pepper

1 cup water

2 tablespoons toasted sesame oil

1 tablespoon minced fresh ginger

1 tablespoon low-sodium soy sauce

½ teaspoon kosher salt

1 teaspoon black pepper

3 cups frozen vegetables (see Note)

¾ cup chopped green onions, for garnish

1. In the Instant Pot, combine the ham, rice, onion, bell pepper, water, sesame oil, ginger, soy sauce, salt, and pepper and stir. Layer the frozen vegetables on top. Do not stir.

2. Secure the lid on the pot. Close the pressure-release valve. Select MANUAL and set the pot at HIGH pressure for 4 minutes. At the end of the cooking time, allow the pot to sit undisturbed for 10 minutes, then release any remaining pressure.

3. Stir to combine. Garnish with the green onions and serve.

NOTE: You can use any combination of vegetables you like—such as 1 cup each peas, corn, and broccoli florets.

PER SERVING

Calories: 290
Total Fat: 9g
Saturated Fat: 2g
Sodium: 710mg
Carbohydrates: 36g
Fiber: 4g
Sugars: 5g
Protein: 15g

BRAISED BEEF SHORT RIBS

You could make this with any kind of meat, really, because it's all about the flavors in the sauce. Smoky, spicy, and very easy. I like to serve this over rice, but I also use it shredded in quesadillas or tacos.

ACTIVE TIME	FUNCTION	RELEASE	TOTAL TIME
20 minutes	Sauté (High); Manual (High)	Natural/Quick	55 minutes

Egg-Free • Nut-Free • Dairy-Free • Gluten-Free • Grain-Free • Soy-Free • Low-Carb • SERVES 4

1 cup chopped onion

1 cup stemmed, seeded, and roughly chopped green bell pepper

1 cup chopped tomatoes

4 to 6 cloves garlic, peeled

1 canned chipotle chile with 1 tablespoon adobo sauce

1 teaspoon dried thyme

1 teaspoon kosher salt

1 teaspoon black pepper

½ teaspoon allspice

2 tablespoons vegetable oil

¾ cup water, divided

2 pounds beef short ribs

1. In a blender or food processor, combine the onion, bell pepper, tomatoes, garlic, chipotle chile, thyme, salt, pepper, and allspice. Blend until well incorporated.

2. Select SAUTÉ/High on the Instant Pot. When the pot is hot, add the oil. Once the oil is hot, add the blended mixture. Cook, stirring frequently, until the water has mostly evaporated, 8 to 10 minutes. Add ¼ cup of the water to deglaze the pot, scraping up the browned bits and allowing the water to evaporate. Add the ribs and the remaining ½ cup water, and stir to combine.

3. Secure the lid on the pot. Close the pressure-release valve. Select MANUAL and set the pot at HIGH pressure for 15 minutes. At the end of the cooking time, allow the pot to sit undisturbed for 10 minutes, then release any remaining pressure.

4. Serve the ribs with the sauce on the side.

PER SERVING		
Calories: 260	Sodium: 580mg	Sugars: 4g
Total Fat: 17g	Carbohydrates: 9g	Protein: 19g
Saturated Fat: 5g	Fiber: 2g	

CHIPOTLE-ORANGE PORK

It's really hard to not overcook pork tenderloin in the Instant Pot. What works for me is 0 minutes at HIGH pressure and a 5- to 10-minute natural-pressure release. When you combine that with a thick and flavorful sauce, you have a really quick dinner.

ACTIVE TIME	FUNCTION	RELEASE	TOTAL TIME
10 minutes	Manual (High); Sauté (Normal)	Natural/Quick	30 minutes

Egg-Free • Nut-Free • Dairy-Free • Gluten-Free • Grain-Free • Soy-Free •
30 Minutes or Less • SERVES 4

¼ cup orange marmalade (see Notes)

1 canned chipotle chile in adobo sauce

1 teaspoon kosher salt

1 teaspoon black pepper

½ teaspoon ground cumin

2 tablespoons plus ¼ cup water, divided

1 cup sliced onion

1 cup dried apricots (see Notes)

1 pound pork tenderloin, cut into thirds

Orange zest and parsley for garnish (optional)

PER SERVING

Calories: 260
Total Fat: 3g
Saturated Fat: 1g
Sodium: 590mg
Carbohydrates: 37g
Fiber: 3g
Sugars: 31g
Protein: 25g

1. In a small blender, combine the marmalade, chipotle chile, salt, pepper, cumin, and the 2 tablespoons water. Blend until almost smooth.

2. In the Instant Pot, combine the ¼ cup water, onion, and apricots, if using. Place the pork on top and pour the sauce over everything. Do not stir.

3. Secure the lid on the pot. Close the pressure-release valve. Select MANUAL and set the pot at HIGH pressure for 0 minutes. At the end of the cooking time, allow the pot to sit undisturbed for 10 minutes, then release any remaining pressure.

4. Remove the pork from the pot and allow it rest for 5 minutes.

5. Slice the pork into medallions and arrange on a serving platter. Sprinkle with orange zest and parsley, if desired. Pour some of the sauce on the pork and pass the rest around at the table.

NOTES: To make this dish low carb, use sugar-free marmalade and do not use the apricots.

You may also want to thicken the sauce with a cornstarch slurry. While the pork is resting, combine ¼ cup water and 1 tablespoon cornstarch in a small bowl. Select SAUTÉ/Normal on the pot. Stir the slurry into the sauce and allow to bubble. Cook, stirring frequently, until thickened, 1 to 2 minutes.

CLASSIC POT ROAST

This one is easy and faster than most other pot roast recipes mainly because the roast is cut into three smaller pieces. Why cook one large roast, have it take forever, and cook unevenly, only to shred it later? #ruthlessefficiency, people!

ACTIVE TIME	FUNCTION	RELEASE	TOTAL TIME
15 minutes	Manual (High)	Natural/Quick	1 hour 5 minutes

Egg-Free • Nut-Free • Dairy-Free • SERVES 8

1 (3-pound) chuck roast, trimmed and cut into thirds

1 cup diced onions

2 tablespoons tomato paste

1 tablespoon Worcestershire sauce

1 teaspoon dried rosemary

1 teaspoon dried thyme

1 teaspoon kosher salt

1 teaspoon black pepper

1½ cups low-sodium beef broth

2 cups chopped carrots

2 cups pearl onions or 1 white onion, coarsely chopped

1½ cups chopped long white potatoes

2 stalks of celery, cut into large pieces

1 cup quartered mushrooms

1. Place the roast in the Instant Pot.

2. In a blender, combine the diced onions, tomato paste, Worcestershire sauce, rosemary, thyme, salt, pepper, and broth. Blend until smooth. Pour the sauce over the roast.

3. Secure the lid on the pot. Close the pressure-release valve. Select MANUAL and set the pot at HIGH pressure for 15 minutes. At the end of the cooking time, use a quick release to depressurize.

4. Open the lid, and stir in the carrots, pearl onions, potatoes, celery, and mushrooms. Secure the lid on the pot. Close the pressure-release valve. Select MANUAL and set the pot at HIGH pressure for 4 minutes. At the end of the cooking time, allow the pot to sit undisturbed for 10 minutes, then release any remaining pressure.

5. Carefully transfer the roast to a bowl and coarsely shred it, then transfer onto a serving platter. Arrange the vegetables around the meat.

6. Serve the pot liquid as a sauce on the side.

PER SERVING		
Calories: 250	Sodium: 420mg	Sugars: 5g
Total Fat: 5g	Carbohydrates: 15g	Protein: 34g
Saturated Fat: 2g	Fiber: 3g	

HEARTY BEEF STEW

I had this recipe on my blog for several years, and one day I took it down because (I thought) every blogger and her cat has a beef stew recipe. Well, I was swamped within a day or two with requests for the recipe. So back up it went! Not only do I use spices that enrich the stew, but because the meat and vegetables are cooked in two cycles, both are perfectly done.

ACTIVE TIME	FUNCTION	RELEASE	TOTAL TIME
15 minutes	Manual (High); Sauté (Normal)	Natural/Quick	1 hour 5 minutes

Egg-Free • Nut-Free • Dairy-Free • SERVES 4

1 pound beef stew meat

1 yellow onion, chopped

1 tablespoon tomato paste

1 tablespoon Worcestershire sauce

1 to 2 teaspoons black pepper

1 teaspoon kosher salt

1 teaspoon smoked paprika

½ teaspoon dried oregano

¾ cup water, divided

2 bay leaves

2 cups sliced mushrooms

2 cups chopped long white potatoes

1 cup baby carrots

1 tablespoon cornstarch or 2 teaspoons arrowroot powder

1. In the Instant Pot, combine the stew meat, onion, tomato paste, Worcestershire sauce, pepper, salt, paprika, oregano, ½ cup of the water, and bay leaves. Stir well.

2. Secure the lid on the pot. Close the pressure-release valve. Select MANUAL and set the pot at HIGH pressure for 15 minutes. At the end of the cooking time, use a quick release to depressurize.

3. Open the lid and stir in the mushrooms, potatoes, and carrots. Secure the lid on the pot. Close the pressure-release valve. Select MANUAL and set the pot at HIGH pressure for 2 minutes. At the end of the cooking time, allow the pot to sit undisturbed for 10 minutes, then release any remaining pressure. Remove the bay leaves and discard.

4. Select SAUTÉ/Normal on the pot. In a small bowl, mix the cornstarch and the remaining ¼ cup water to make a slurry. Stir the slurry into the stew and allow to bubble. Cook, stirring frequently, until thickened, 3 to 5 minutes.

PER SERVING

Calories: 260
Total Fat: 8g
Saturated Fat: 3g

Sodium: 600mg
Carbohydrates: 22g
Fiber: 3g

Sugars: 4g
Protein: 25g

IRISH LAMB STEW

I spoke to several people about this recipe before making it, and I was very skeptical about the rather sparse list of seasonings they all advised me to use. But lamb makes such a rich and comforting broth that you really don't want to hide it under a lot of other flavors.

ACTIVE TIME	FUNCTION	RELEASE	TOTAL TIME
15 minutes	Sauté (Normal); Manual (High)	Natural/Quick	1 hour

Egg-Free • Nut-Free • Dairy-Free • Gluten-Free • Soy-Free • SERVES 6

2 tablespoons vegetable oil

3 cloves garlic, minced

1 pound boneless leg of lamb, cut into 2-inch cubes

2 large onions, cut into large wedges

2 bay leaves

1½ teaspoons kosher salt

1½ teaspoons black pepper

2½ cups plus 2 tablespoons water, divided

1 tablespoon cornstarch

1 leek, sliced (white and light green parts)

2 cups halved baby yellow or red potatoes

4 large carrots, cut into 2-inch pieces

2 turnips, cut into 2-inch chunks (optional)

¼ cup chopped fresh parsley

1. Select SAUTÉ/Normal on the Instant Pot. When the pot is hot, add the oil. Once the oil is hot, add the garlic and stir. Select CANCEL. Add the lamb, onions, bay leaves, salt, pepper, and the 2½ cups water.

2. Secure the lid on the pot. Close the pressure-release valve. Select MANUAL and set the pot at HIGH pressure for 10 minutes. At the end of the cooking time, use a quick release to depressurize.

3. In a small bowl, mix the cornstarch and the 2 tablespoons water to make a slurry. Stir the slurry into the pot and allow to bubble.

4. Add the leeks, potatoes, carrots, and turnips, if using.

5. Secure the lid on the pot. Close the pressure-release valve. Select MANUAL and set the pot at HIGH pressure for 5 minutes. At the end of the cooking time, allow the pot to sit undisturbed for 10 minutes, then release any remaining pressure.

6. Discard the bay leaves, garnish with parsley, and serve.

PER SERVING

Calories: 290	Sodium: 570mg	Sugars: 6g
Total Fat: 16g	Carbohydrates: 21g	Protein: 16g
Saturated Fat: 5g	Fiber: 3g	

PAPRIKA PORK CHOPS WITH CABBAGE

The cabbage cooks down quite a bit in this dish, so if you like your cabbage crunchy, just cut it into large chunks or quarters. If you want a more tender texture, cut up that cabbage and enjoy an easy dinner with lots of flavor.

ACTIVE TIME	FUNCTION	RELEASE	TOTAL TIME
15 minutes	Sauté (High); Manual (High)	Natural/Quick	35 minutes

Egg-Free • Nut-Free • Gluten-Free • Grain-Free • Soy-Free • Low-Carb • SERVES 4

1 tablespoon vegetable oil

1 teaspoon caraway seeds

1 teaspoon smoked paprika

1 teaspoon kosher salt

1 teaspoon black pepper

1 cup sliced onion

1 cup sliced mushrooms

¼ cup water

4 (1½-inch-thick) boneless lean pork chops (8 ounces each)

4 cups sliced (1-inch) cabbage

½ cup sour cream (see Note)

¼ cup chopped fresh parsley

PER SERVING

Calories: 400
Total Fat: 16g
Saturated Fat: 5g
Sodium: 710mg
Carbohydrates: 10g
Fiber: 3g
Sugars: 5g
Protein: 57g

1. Select SAUTÉ/High on the Instant Pot. When the pot is hot, add the oil. Once the oil is hot, add the caraway seeds, and let sizzle for 15 to 20 seconds. Add the paprika, salt, and pepper and stir. Add the onion and mushrooms and stir to coat.

2. Stir in the water and place the pork chops on top of the vegetables. Add the cabbage on top of the pork chops.

3. Secure the lid on the pot. Close the pressure-release valve. Select MANUAL and set the pot at HIGH pressure for 4 minutes. At the end of the cooking time, allow the pot to sit undisturbed for 5 minutes, then release any remaining pressure.

4. Remove the cabbage and pork chops from the pot.

5. Stir in the sour cream.

6. Serve the sauce over the pork chops. Garnish with parsley before serving.

NOTE: For a dairy-free option, omit the sour cream. If you omit the sour cream, you may want to thicken the sauce with a cornstarch slurry. To make the slurry, in a small bowl, mix 1 tablespoon cornstarch and ¼ cup water. Select SAUTÉ/Normal after the pressure is released. Stir the slurry into the pot and allow to bubble. Cook, stirring frequently, until thickened, 3 to 5 minutes.

NEW ENGLAND BOILED DINNER

Two tips to make this perfect and fast: Cut up that corned beef so that all of it cooks evenly and fast. And don't try to make the vegetables and beef in one go unless you want total mush. Other than that, it's a super-simple recipe that makes tasty leftovers.

ACTIVE TIME	FUNCTION	RELEASE	TOTAL TIME
15 minutes	Manual (High)	Natural/Quick	1 hour 35 minutes

Egg-Free · Nut-Free · Dairy-Free · Gluten-Free · Grain-Free · Soy-Free · Low-Carb · SERVES 8

1½ cups water

4 pounds corned beef, trimmed, with spice packet

16 baby potatoes

3 cups baby carrots

2 onions, quartered

1 head cabbage, quartered

Black pepper

PER SERVING

Calories: 320
Total Fat: 16g
Saturated Fat: 5g
Sodium: 890mg
Carbohydrates: 27g
Fiber: 5g
Sugars: 6g
Protein: 19g

---

1. Pour the water into the Instant Pot. Cut the corned beef in half at its thickest part and place in the pot. Sprinkle the contents of the spice packet over the meat.

2. Secure the lid on the pot. Close the pressure-release valve. Select MANUAL and set the pot at HIGH pressure for 60 minutes. At the end of the cooking time, allow the pot to sit undisturbed for 10 minutes, then release any remaining pressure.

3. Place the potatoes, carrots, and onions on top of the corned beef. Arrange the cabbage on top. Do not stir. Secure the lid on the pot. Close the pressure-release valve. Select MANUAL and set the pot at HIGH pressure for 5 minutes. At the end of the cooking time, allow the pot to sit undisturbed for 10 minutes, then release any remaining pressure.

4. Transfer the vegetables to half of a large serving dish. Remove the corned beef and slice. Arrange the slices on the other half of the dish. Season everything to taste with pepper and serve.

ONE-POT BIBIMBAP

Trying to figure this one out kept me awake many nights. I really, really wanted to figure out a one-pot bibimbap because I love eating it but can't be bothered to make five items separately. Once you consider that everything is getting mixed up before eating anyway, it makes sense to make it in one go. After fussing with making things pot-in-pot, I realized this one-pot method works the best.

ACTIVE TIME	FUNCTION	RELEASE	TOTAL TIME
20 minutes	Sauté (Normal); Manual (High)	Natural/Quick	45 minutes

Egg-Free • Nut-Free • Dairy-Free • SERVES 4

For the Sauce

2 tablespoons gochujang (Korean red chile paste)

1 tablespoon low-sodium soy sauce

1 tablespoon toasted sesame oil

1 tablespoon sugar

1 tablespoon rice vinegar

1 clove garlic, minced

2 tablespoons water

For the Vegetables

3 cups stemmed spinach leaves

1 tablespoon sesame oil

½ teaspoon kosher salt

2 cups shredded carrots

1 cup bean sprouts

For the Main Dish

8 ounces (90% lean) ground beef

1¼ cups water, divided

1 cup jasmine rice, rinsed and drained

1. **For the Sauce:** In a medium bowl, combine the gochujang, soy sauce, sesame oil, sugar, vinegar, garlic, and water and whisk well.

2. **For the Vegetables:** In a large bowl, combine the spinach, sesame oil, and salt. Use your hands to roughly massage the spinach. Add the carrots and bean sprouts and gently mix. Place the vegetables in the center of a large sheet of aluminum foil. Bring the two ends of the foil together and roll down toward the vegetables. Roll up the sides of the packet to enclose the vegetables.

3. **For the Main Dish:** Select SAUTÉ/Normal on the Instant Pot. When the pot is hot, add the ground beef and break it up with a wooden spoon, 2 to 3 minutes. Stir in ¼ cup of the water and allow it to completely evaporate.

4. Add the rice, soy sauce, sesame oil, garlic, and salt. Stir well. Add the mushrooms and the remaining 1 cup water. Select CANCEL.

5. Place a tall trivet in the pot. Set the foil packet on the trivet.

6. Secure the lid on the pot. Close the pressure-release valve. Select MANUAL and set the pot at HIGH pressure for 4 minutes.

recipe continues

1 tablespoon low-sodium soy sauce

1 tablespoon toasted sesame oil

2 cloves garlic, minced

½ teaspoon kosher salt

1 cup sliced mushrooms

4 fried eggs, for serving (optional)

PER SERVING

Calories: 410
Total Fat: 16g
Saturated Fat: 4g
Sodium: 710mg
Carbohydrates: 51g
Fiber: 2g
Sugars: 9g
Protein: 18g

At the end of the cooking time, allow the pot to sit undisturbed for 10 minutes, then release any remaining pressure.

7. Carefully remove the foil packet and gently stir the vegetables and their cooking liquid into the rice mixture.

8. Divide the mixture among four shallow serving bowls. Top each serving with a fried egg, if desired. Serve with the sauce.

SAUERKRAUT, POTATOES, AND SAUSAGE

When I make this very simple and tasty soup, I like to reserve a little sauerkraut juice to add later—not just for the added tang but also to get some of those healthy probiotics into my soup and tummy. This soup keeps well for several days and freezes well.

ACTIVE TIME	FUNCTION	RELEASE	TOTAL TIME
5 minutes	Manual (High)	Natural/Quick	25 minutes

Egg-Free • Nut-Free • Dairy-Free • Gluten-Free • Grain-Free • Soy-Free • Low-Carb • 30 Minutes or Less • SERVES 4

2 cups sauerkraut, with brine

2 cups baby potatoes, halved

1 cup sliced onion

3 whole cloves

½ teaspoon black pepper

⅓ cup water

12 ounces fresh or cooked sausage (see Note)

PER SERVING

Calories: 270
Total Fat: 16g
Saturated Fat: 6g
Sodium: 1,210mg
Carbohydrates: 25g
Fiber: 5g
Sugars: 4g
Protein: 9g

1. In the Instant Pot, combine the sauerkraut, potatoes, onion, cloves, pepper, and water. Stir well. Place the sausage on top.

2. Secure the lid on the pot. Close the pressure-release valve. Select MANUAL and set the pot at HIGH pressure for 2 minutes. At the end of the cooking time, allow the pot to sit undisturbed for 5 minutes, then release any remaining pressure.

3. Open the lid, discard the cloves, and serve.

NOTE: If you're using smoked sausage, cut the sausage into 4-inch pieces. If you're using fresh sausage, leave it whole. For a lower-carb variation, increase the sausage to 1 pound, omit the potatoes, and reduce the water to ¼ cup.

PORK BELLY AND BOK CHOY NOODLE SOUP

You are essentially making a quick and flavorful pork broth in the first step of this recipe. Using pork belly allows you to incorporate some of the fat into the broth, which makes the final product similar to a ramen broth. You can also make this soup with 1 pound diced boneless skinless chicken thighs without changing ingredients or cook time.

ACTIVE TIME	FUNCTION	RELEASE	TOTAL TIME
10 minutes	Manual (High)	Natural/Quick	45 minutes

Egg-Free • Nut-Free • Dairy-Free • SERVES 4

8 ounces pork belly, cut into thin slices

3 cups low-sodium chicken broth

2 tablespoons low-sodium soy sauce

1 tablespoon minced fresh ginger

½ teaspoon kosher salt

3 cups baby bok choy, chopped

4 ounces dried rice noodles

1 cup chopped green onions

PER SERVING

Calories: 450
Total Fat: 31g
Saturated Fat: 11g
Sodium: 620mg
Carbohydrates: 29g
Fiber: 2g
Sugars: 2g
Protein: 12g

1. In the Instant Pot, combine the pork belly, broth, soy sauce, ginger, and salt.

2. Secure the lid on the pot. Close the pressure-release valve. Select MANUAL and set the pot at HIGH pressure for 10 minutes. At the end of the cooking time, allow the pot to sit undisturbed for 5 minutes, then release any remaining pressure.

3. Open the lid, and stir in the bok choy and noodles. Close the lid, and allow the bok choy and noodles to cook in the residual heat, about 10 minutes.

4. Stir in the green onions and serve.

RENDANG-STYLE BEEF AND POTATOES

Malaysian rendang is a time-consuming but utterly delicious way to cook beef. I have a cheater version of this on my blog, but that one uses a packet of seasoning—one of the few times I do that! For this book, I wanted something that was close enough to rendang but without a ton of the ingredients that typically go into the paste. Hence, we have "rendang-style." Adding the potatoes makes it heartier, and you can either have it with a side of veggies or add some rice—because carbs and deliciousness!

ACTIVE TIME	FUNCTION	RELEASE	TOTAL TIME
10 minutes	Manual (High)	Natural/Quick	1 hour 15 minutes

Egg-Free • Nut-Free • Dairy-Free • Gluten-Free • Grain-Free • Soy-Free • SERVES 8

2 pounds boneless beef chuck

1 cup chopped onion

1 (14-ounce) can full-fat coconut milk, divided

4 cloves garlic, peeled

2 tablespoons finely chopped fresh ginger

3 tablespoons fresh lime juice, divided

1½ teaspoons kosher salt

1 teaspoon cinnamon

1 teaspoon ground turmeric

½ teaspoon ground cloves

½ teaspoon ground nutmeg

½ teaspoon cayenne pepper

½ cup water, divided

3 cups chopped (¾-inch) long white potatoes

¼ cup chopped fresh cilantro

1. Cut the beef into 2-inch pieces. Place the beef cubes in a resealable plastic bag or a large mixing bowl.

2. In a small blender, combine the onion, ⅓ cup of the coconut milk, garlic, ginger, 2 tablespoons of the lime juice, salt, cinnamon, turmeric, cloves, nutmeg, and cayenne. Blend until you have a smooth paste.

3. Add the marinade to the resealable plastic bag with the beef cubes. Use ¼ cup of the water to rinse out the blender, and add to the bag. Seal, and massage until all of the beef is well coated. Marinate at room temperature for 30 minutes or in the refrigerator for up to 48 hours.

4. When you are ready to cook, place the beef and marinade into the Instant Pot. Pour the remaining ¼ cup water into the pot.

5. Secure the lid on the pot. Close the pressure-release valve. Select MANUAL and set the pot at HIGH pressure for 20 minutes. At the end of the cooking time, allow the pot to sit undisturbed for 10 minutes, then release any remaining pressure.

6. Open the lid and add the potatoes. Secure the lid on the pot. Close the pressure-release valve. Select MANUAL and set the pot at HIGH pressure for 3 minutes. At the end of the cooking time, allow the pot to sit undisturbed for 5 minutes, then release any remaining pressure.

7. Stir in the remaining coconut milk, the remaining 1 tablespoon lime juice, and cilantro and serve.

SAUSAGE, POTATO, AND KALE SOUP

This recipe calls for just a half-pound of sausage and lots of vegetables to fill out the soup—but you can always use more sausage if you like. You can use vegetable or olive oil for the first step, but save your best olive oil to drizzle on top.

ACTIVE TIME	FUNCTION	RELEASE	TOTAL TIME
10 minutes	Sauté (Normal); Manual (High)	Natural/Quick	35 minutes

Egg-Free · Nut-Free · Dairy-Free · Gluten-Free · Grain-Free · Soy-Free · SERVES 4

2 tablespoons vegetable oil or extra-virgin olive oil

8 ounces reduced-fat smoked sausage, sliced

1½ cups diced onion

3 cloves garlic, minced

3 cups chopped long white potatoes

4 cups low-sodium chicken broth or water

1 teaspoon kosher salt

1 teaspoon black pepper

6 cups chopped fresh kale

Hot extra-virgin olive oil, for drizzling

1. Select SAUTÉ/Normal on the Instant Pot. When the pot is hot, add the oil, sausage, onion, and garlic. Cook, stirring frequently, until the onion softens, 1 to 2 minutes. Select CANCEL.

2. Add the potatoes, broth, salt, and pepper and stir well to combine. Place the kale on top. Do not stir.

3. Secure the lid on the pot. Close the pressure-release valve. Select MANUAL and set the pot at HIGH pressure for 3 minutes. At the end of the cooking time, allow the pot to sit undisturbed for 10 minutes, then release any remaining pressure.

4. Using the back of a wooden spoon, mash about half of the potatoes to thicken the broth.

5. Divide the soup among four serving bowls. Drizzle each serving with hot olive oil.

PER SERVING

Calories: 320
Total Fat: 11g
Saturated Fat: 2g

Sodium: 1,050mg
Carbohydrates: 44g
Fiber: 8g

Sugars: 6g
Protein: 17g

SHREDDED PORK TACOS

Super simple but very flavorful shredded pork tacos can now be a weeknight dinner. I used boneless county-style ribs, which are nothing more than cut-up pork shoulder and are easy to buy in small amounts. But if you'd rather use pork shoulder (also called pork butt), just cut up the meat to resemble country ribs (3- to 4-inch-thick slices) and cook as directed.

ACTIVE TIME	FUNCTION	RELEASE	TOTAL TIME
15 minutes	Manual (High)	Natural/Quick	1 hour 20 minutes

Egg-Free • Nut-Free • Dairy-Free • Gluten-Free • Grain-Free • Soy-Free • Low-Carb • SERVES 8

1 cup chopped onion

1 cup stemmed, seeded, and roughly chopped green, yellow, or orange bell pepper

6 cloves garlic, peeled

2 tablespoons vegetable oil

2 tablespoons fresh lemon juice

1½ teaspoons ground cumin

1½ teaspoons kosher salt

1 teaspoon dried oregano

2 pounds lean boneless country-style pork ribs

Corn or flour tortillas (see Note)

Optional toppings:
Diced tomatoes, chopped fresh cilantro, diced roasted jalapeños

PER SERVING

Calories: 220
Total Fat: 13g
Saturated Fat: 4g
Sodium: 400mg

Carbohydrates: 4g
Fiber: 1g
Sugars: 1g
Protein: 20g

1. In a blender, combine the onion, bell pepper, garlic, oil, lemon juice, cumin, salt, and oregano. Blend until smooth. Place the pork in a resealable plastic bag. Add the marinade, seal, and massage until the pork is well coated. Marinate at room temperature for 30 minutes or in the refrigerator overnight.

2. When you are ready to cook, transfer the pork and marinade to the Instant Pot. (The liquid should be about ½ cup. If you do not have enough, add a little water to the pot.)

3. Secure the lid on the pot. Close the pressure-release valve. Select MANUAL and set the pot at HIGH pressure for 30 minutes. At the end of the cooking time, allow the pot to sit undisturbed for 10 minutes, then release any remaining pressure.

4. Carefully transfer the pork to a bowl and shred it. Moisten with the sauce from the pot as desired.

5. Serve in tortillas with desired toppings.

NOTE: For a lower-carb option, omit the tortillas and serve over spinach or shredded cabbage. Sometimes I use the leftover pork in a casserole. To do this, prepare an 8-ounce package of cornbread mix as directed. Place the shredded pork and ½ cup of the cooking liquid in the bottom of a baking dish. Pour the cornbread mix on top, and bake at 350°F for 15 to 20 minutes, until the cornbread is cooked through.

SPICY BEEF BARBACOA

I call this my Better-Than-Chipotle Barbacoa, and when you make it, you will see exactly why. This was a huge hit in my Facebook group, where I posted it as a sneak peek for everyone. I wrote this for one pound of meat because many of us can't finish several pounds of meat at once, but you can always double or triple the recipe. If you do that, double or triple everything except the water. You can freeze the leftovers along with some of the cooking liquid to keep it moist when defrosting.

ACTIVE TIME	FUNCTION	RELEASE	TOTAL TIME
10 minutes	Manual (High)	Natural/Quick	50 minutes

Egg-Free • Nut-Free • Dairy-Free • Gluten-Free • Grain-Free • Soy-Free • Low-Carb • SERVES 6

6 cloves garlic, peeled

1 tablespoon ground cumin

3 tablespoons apple cider vinegar

1 canned chipotle chile in adobo sauce

2 teaspoons dried oregano

1 teaspoon kosher salt

1 tablespoon Mexican red chile powder

¼ teaspoon ground cloves

1 cup water

1 pound beef chuck roast, cut into 5 to 6 pieces

2 tablespoons fresh lime juice

PER SERVING

Calories: 90
Total Fat: 2g
Saturated Fat: 1g
Sodium: 400mg
Carbohydrates: 2g
Fiber: 0g
Sugars: 0g
Protein: 14g

1. In a small blender, combine the garlic, cumin, vinegar, chipotle chile, oregano, salt, chile powder, cloves, and water. Blend until well incorporated. Transfer the mixture to the Instant Pot and add the beef.

2. Secure the lid on the pot. Close the pressure-release valve. Select MANUAL and set the pot at HIGH pressure for 30 minutes. At the end of the cooking time, allow the pot to sit undisturbed for 10 minutes, then release any remaining pressure.

3. Carefully transfer the beef to a cutting board. Using two forks, shred the beef. Return the beef to the pot. Stir in the lime juice.

SERVING SUGGESTIONS

As a salad: Serve the meat on a bed of chopped romaine lettuce topped with sour cream, salsa, guacamole, chopped red onions, and cilantro. Drizzle with additional cooking liquid.

Tacos: Wrap in corn or flour tortillas with chopped red onions and cilantro.

Over rice: Cook brown rice in the same pot as the meat.

SPLIT PEAS AND HAM

Allow this to rest for the whole ten minutes before you release the pressure. If you see any foaming or pea-spurting happening, close that valve and give it another five minutes. This soup thickens as it stands, so you may need to add a little more water.

ACTIVE TIME	FUNCTION	RELEASE	TOTAL TIME
5 minutes	Manual (High)	Natural/Quick	45 minutes

Egg-Free • Nut-Free • Dairy-Free • Gluten-Free • Grain-Free • Soy-Free • SERVES 4

2 cups diced low-sodium ham

2 cups frozen mirepoix (diced onions, celery, and carrot)

2 cups water

1 cup dried green split peas

1 teaspoon kosher salt

1 teaspoon black pepper

2 bay leaves

1 to 2 tablespoons Louisiana hot sauce

3 tablespoons apple cider vinegar

2 teaspoons liquid smoke

1. In the Instant Pot, combine the ham, mirepoix, water, split peas, salt, pepper, and bay leaves.

2. Secure the lid on the pot. Close the pressure-release valve. Select MANUAL and set the pot at HIGH pressure for 20 minutes. At the end of the cooking time, allow the pot to sit undisturbed for 10 minutes, then release any remaining pressure.

3. Open the lid, stir in the hot sauce, vinegar, and liquid smoke. Discard the bay leaves and serve.

PER SERVING

Calories: 310
Total Fat: 6g
Saturated Fat: 2g
Sodium: 1,300mg
Carbohydrates: 36g
Fiber: 14g
Sugars: 6g
Protein: 28g

VIETNAMESE BEEF STEW

Your house is going to smell SO GOOD when you make this stew! It took me a few tries to get this right, because I wanted a one-cycle cooking time for this. But unless you put the veggies in a pot inside the Instant Pot, all you get is mush. Done this way, though, it will be perfect.

ACTIVE TIME	FUNCTION	RELEASE	TOTAL TIME
10 minutes	Manual (High); Sauté (Normal)	Natural/Quick	50 minutes

Egg-Free • Nut-Free • Dairy-Free • Gluten-Free • Soy-Free • SERVES 4

1 pound beef stew meat

1 onion, chopped

2 tablespoons tomato paste

1 tablespoon lemongrass paste

3 cloves garlic, minced

2 whole star anise

1 tablespoon minced fresh ginger

1 teaspoon black pepper

½ teaspoon Chinese five-spice powder

½ teaspoon curry powder

1 teaspoon kosher salt

1¾ cups water, divided

2 carrots, cut into 3-inch pieces

2 long white potatoes, cut into 3-inch pieces

1 turnip, trimmed, peeled, and quartered

1 tablespoon cornstarch

1. In the Instant Pot, combine the beef, onion, tomato paste, lemongrass paste, garlic, star anise, ginger, pepper, five-spice powder, curry powder, salt, and 1½ cups of the water.

2. Place the carrots, potatoes, and turnip in a 7 × 3-inch round heatproof pan. Place a trivet in the pot. Set the pan with the vegetables on the trivet.

3. Secure the lid on the pot. Close the pressure-release valve. Select MANUAL and set the pot at HIGH pressure for 15 minutes. At the end of the cooking time, allow the pot to sit undisturbed for 10 minutes, then release any remaining pressure.

4. Remove the vegetables and cut smaller, if desired, before adding to the stew.

5. Select SAUTÉ/Normal on the pot. In a small bowl, mix the cornstarch and the remaining ¼ cup water to make a slurry. Stir the slurry into the stew and allow to bubble. Cook, stirring frequently, until thickened, about 2 minutes.

PER SERVING

Calories: 300
Total Fat: 9g
Saturated Fat: 3g

Sodium: 650mg
Carbohydrates: 31g
Fiber: 4g

Sugars: 5g
Protein: 25g

SWEET-AND-SOUR STEAK AND CABBAGE STEW

Yes, this recipe does indeed call for a tiny bit of sweetener. That's the sweet part of the sweet and sour. Just keep in mind that it's a few teaspoons spread across six servings, so it's not a lot.

ACTIVE TIME	FUNCTION	RELEASE	TOTAL TIME
10 minutes	Manual (High)	Natural/Quick	30 minutes

Egg-Free • Nut-Free • Dairy-Free • Low-Carb • 30 Minutes or Less • SERVES 6

2 tablespoons tomato paste

2 tablespoons Worcestershire sauce

2 teaspoons cornstarch

2 teaspoons dried thyme

1 teaspoon kosher salt

1 teaspoon black pepper

2 to 3 teaspoons sugar or honey, or 1 teaspoon Splenda or Truvia

3 cups low-sodium beef broth

1 pound flank steak, cut into large bite-size chunks

3 cups baby potatoes (see Note)

1 cup diced onion

3 cups chopped green cabbage

¼ cup chopped fresh parsley

2 tablespoons apple cider vinegar

1. In the Instant Pot, combine the tomato paste, Worcestershire sauce, cornstarch, thyme, salt, pepper, sugar, and broth. Whisk until there are no lumps of cornstarch. Add the steak, potatoes, and onion. Place the cabbage on top. Do not stir.

2. Secure the lid on the pot. Close the pressure-release valve. Select MANUAL and set the pot at HIGH pressure for 2 minutes. At the end of the cooking time, allow the pot to sit undisturbed for 5 minutes, then release any remaining pressure.

3. Stir in the parsley and vinegar and serve.

NOTE: For a low-carb option, substitute 3 cups large turnip chunks for the baby potatoes.

PER SERVING

Calories: 220
Total Fat: 5g
Saturated Fat: 2g
Sodium: 470mg
Carbohydrates: 22g
Fiber: 3g
Sugars: 6g
Protein: 21g

TEXAS-STYLE CHILI

I've included this chili in my *Keto Instant Pot Cookbook* as well. I try not to repeat recipes, but this one is a repeat chili cook-off champion, and I want you to be a winner—even if it is only at your own dinner table! if it is only at your own dinner table.

ACTIVE TIME	FUNCTION	RELEASE	TOTAL TIME
10 minutes	Sauté (Normal); Manual (High)	Natural/Quick	40 minutes

Egg-Free • Nut-Free • Dairy-Free • Soy-Free • Low-Carb • SERVES 4

1 cup canned fire-roasted tomatoes

1 tablespoon chopped canned chipotle chile in adobo sauce

2 corn tortillas

1 tablespoon vegetable oil

1 cup chopped onion

3 cloves garlic, minced

1 pound 90% lean ground beef

3 teaspoons Mexican red chile powder

2 teaspoons ground cumin

1½ teaspoons kosher salt

1 teaspoon dried oregano

½ cup water

Shredded cheddar cheese or shredded Mexican cheese blend (optional)

1. In a blender, combine the tomatoes, chipotle chile, and tortillas. Blend until smooth.

2. Select SAUTÉ/Normal on the Instant Pot. When the pot is hot, add the oil. Once the oil is hot, add the onion and garlic. Cook, stirring frequently, for 30 seconds. Add the ground beef and break up with a wooden spoon.

3. Add the chile powder, cumin, salt, and oregano. Allow the spices to bloom, about 30 seconds. Add the blender mixture. Rinse the blender using the water, and pour that into the pot.

4. Secure the lid on the pot. Close the pressure-release valve. Select MANUAL and set the pot at HIGH pressure for 10 minutes. At the end of the cooking time, allow the pot to sit undisturbed for 10 minutes, then release any remaining pressure.

5. Stir well to combine.

6. Top servings with shredded cheese, if desired.

PER SERVING

Calories: 260
Total Fat: 13g
Saturated Fat: 4g
Sodium: 990mg
Carbohydrates: 11g
Fiber: 2g
Sugars: 4g
Protein: 23g

WHITE BEAN AND SAUSAGE SOUP

You want a small bean like navy beans for this so that the beans cook down into the soup to thicken it. I used chicken sausage to keep the fat down a little, but if your diet can take a little fat now and then, feel free to use regular Italian sausage.

ACTIVE TIME	FUNCTION	RELEASE	TOTAL TIME
15 minutes	Sauté (Normal); Manual (High)	Natural/Quick	1 hour 5 minutes plus 1 hour soaking time

Egg-Free · Nut-Free · Dairy-Free · Gluten-Free · Grain-Free · Soy-Free · Low-Carb · SERVES 8

1 cup dried navy beans

1 pound bulk Italian-style turkey or chicken sausage

2 cloves garlic, minced

2 cups diced large onions

1 (14.5-ounce) can diced fire-roasted tomatoes

3 to 4 bay leaves

1 tablespoon Italian seasoning

1½ teaspoons kosher salt

3½ cups water

4 cups chopped fresh collard greens

½ cup chopped fresh parsley (optional)

½ cup shredded Parmesan cheese (optional)

1. One hour before you plan to cook, place the dried beans in a bowl and cover with hot water by 2 inches; drain before using.

2. Select SAUTÉ/Normal on the Instant Pot. When the pot is hot, add the sausage and garlic and break up with a wooden spoon. Add the onions, tomatoes, beans, bay leaves, Italian seasoning, salt, and water. Stir in the collard greens.

3. Secure the lid on the pot. Close the pressure-release valve. Select MANUAL and set the pot at HIGH pressure for 35 minutes. At the end of the cooking time, allow the pot to sit undisturbed for 10 minutes, then release any remaining pressure.

4. Discard the bay leaves, stir in parsley and Parmesan cheese (if desired), and serve.

PER SERVING

Calories: 200
Total Fat: 5g
Saturated Fat: 2g
Sodium: 850mg
Carbohydrates: 22g
Fiber: 6g
Sugars: 4g
Protein: 17g

SEAFOOD

BELIZEAN COCONUT AND SEAFOOD SOUP

I run Twosleevers culinary tours where a bunch of us basically go places and eat our way across a country. Yes, it is exactly as much fun as it sounds! So, on the last trip to Belize, we attended a cooking class and were taught how to make *hudut*, which is a Garifuna coconut soup that I've reproduced here. Traditionally, it is served with mashed plantains (which are beaten in a mortar for what feels like HOURS), but I listed rice or cauliflower rice for a low-carb option.

ACTIVE TIME	FUNCTION	RELEASE	TOTAL TIME
10 minutes	Manual (Low)	Natural/Quick	30 minutes

Egg-Free · Nut-Free · Dairy-Free · Gluten-Free · Grain-Free · Soy-Free · Low-Carb · 30 Minutes or Less · SERVES 4

1 pound frozen firm white fish fillets, such as cod, tilapia, or haddock

1 cup thinly sliced onion

3 cloves garlic, minced

2 to 4 thin slices fresh ginger

2 sprigs cilantro

1½ teaspoons kosher salt

1 teaspoon black pepper

1 teaspoon dried oregano

1 teaspoon dried basil

1 teaspoon dried parsley

1½ cups water

1 cup full-fat coconut milk

1 tablespoon fresh lime juice

Steamed white rice or steamed cauliflower rice (optional)

1. In the Instant Pot, combine the fish, onion, garlic, ginger, cilantro, salt, pepper, oregano, basil, parsley, and water.

2. Secure the lid on the pot. Close the pressure-release valve. Select MANUAL and set the pot at LOW pressure for 2 minutes. At the end of the cooking time, allow the pot to sit undisturbed for 5 minutes, then release any remaining pressure.

3. Open the lid, and discard the cilantro stalks and ginger. Gently break the fish into large chunks. Stir in the coconut milk and lime juice and serve with rice, if desired.

PER SERVING

Calories: 230
Total Fat: 13g
Saturated Fat: 11g
Sodium: 790mg
Carbohydrates: 7g
Fiber: 1g
Sugars: 2g
Protein: 22g

CHIMICHURRI FISH AND COUSCOUS

This recipe is so fast! You start with frozen fish, so it requires little to no preplanning. It also works very well with pesto in place of the chimichurri.

ACTIVE TIME	FUNCTION	RELEASE	TOTAL TIME
10 minutes	Manual (High)	Natural/Quick	25 minutes

Egg-Free · Nut-Free · Dairy-Free · Soy-Free · Low-Carb · 30 Minutes or Less · Grain-Free · SERVES 4

½ cup fresh cilantro

½ cup fresh parsley

4 tablespoons extra-virgin olive oil, divided

6 cloves garlic, peeled

½ to 1 teaspoon red pepper flakes

1 pound frozen firm white fish fillets, such as cod, tilapia, or haddock

1 cup Israeli couscous

1 cup water

1 teaspoon kosher salt

1 cup cherry tomatoes

PER SERVING

Calories: 360
Total Fat: 15g
Saturated Fat: 2g
Sodium: 550mg
Carbohydrates: 30g
Fiber: 2g
Sugars: 2g
Protein: 25g

1. Prepare the chimichurri in a blender; combine the cilantro, parsley, 3 tablespoons of the olive oil, garlic, and red pepper flakes. Blend until well combined.

2. In the Instant Pot, combine the couscous, water, remaining 1 tablespoon olive oil, and salt. Place the fillets on top and drizzle with half the chimichurri, reserving the other half for serving. Scatter the cherry tomatoes on top of the fish.

3. Secure the lid on the pot. Close the pressure-release valve. Select MANUAL and set the pot at HIGH pressure for 1 minute. At the end of the cooking time, allow the pot to sit undisturbed for 5 minutes, then release any remaining pressure.

4. Transfer the fish and couscous to a serving platter. Drizzle with the remaining chimichurri and serve.

EASIEST-EVER SHRIMP CURRY

I had this recipe in my first Instant Pot cookbook and it is so simple and so popular, I thought I'd include it in this book as well. I added a few more veggies to this version to round it out a bit. It's important to use thawed shrimp and a metal pan for this. If you only have a glass pan, you may need to increase cooking times.

ACTIVE TIME	FUNCTION	RELEASE	TOTAL TIME
10 minutes	Manual (High)	Quick	25 minutes

Egg-Free • Nut-Free • Dairy-Free • Gluten-Free • Soy-Free • Low-Carb • 30 Minutes or Less • SERVES 4

1½ cups full-fat coconut milk

1 tablespoon minced fresh ginger

3 cloves garlic, minced

1 teaspoon kosher salt

1 teaspoon Garam Masala (page 221)

½ teaspoon ground turmeric

½ teaspoon cayenne pepper

1 pound raw shrimp, shelled and deveined (about 26/30 count)

1 cup stemmed, seeded, and sliced bell pepper (any color or mixed)

1 cup frozen peas, thawed

1½ cups water

Rice, naan, and/or spiralized cucumber

1. In a 6 × 3-inch round heatproof pan, whisk together the coconut milk, ginger, garlic, salt, Garam Masala, turmeric, and cayenne. Add the shrimp and mix gently to coat. Press down on the shrimp to ensure they are mostly submerged. Scatter the bell pepper slices and peas over the shrimp.

2. Pour the water into the Instant Pot. Place a trivet in the pot. Set the pan with the shrimp in it on the trivet.

3. Secure the lid on the pot. Close the pressure-release valve. Select MANUAL and set the pot at HIGH pressure for 3 minutes. At the end of the cooking time, use a quick release to depressurize. Mix well.

4. Serve over rice, naan, or spiralized cucumber.

PER SERVING

Calories: 210
Total Fat: 19g
Saturated Fat: 16g
Sodium: 650mg
Carbohydrates: 10g
Fiber: 4g
Sugars: 2g
Protein: 27g

FISH AND CHARD SOUP

Light and brothy and full of lean protein and veggies—but mainly delicious and fast! This one won't take to multiple reheatings, so make only what you can eat in a day or two. You can switch the Swiss chard for spinach or bok choy without changing cooking times.

ACTIVE TIME	FUNCTION	RELEASE	TOTAL TIME
10 minutes	Sauté (Normal); Manual (High)	Natural/Quick	25 minutes

Egg-Free • Nut-Free • Dairy-Free • Low-Carb • 30 Minutes or Less • SERVES 4

2 tablespoons toasted sesame oil, divided

5 to 6 thin slices fresh ginger

2 cups low-sodium chicken broth

1½ cups sliced mushrooms

1 tablespoon soy sauce

4 cups chopped rainbow Swiss chard

1 pound frozen firm white fish fillets, such as cod, tilapia, or haddock

Sriracha or other hot sauce to taste (optional)

¼ cup chopped green onions (optional)

1. Select SAUTÉ/Normal on the Instant Pot. When the pot is hot, add 1 tablespoon of the sesame oil and ginger, and let sizzle for 10 to 15 seconds.

2. Add the broth, mushrooms, and soy sauce. Stir well. Add the chard, and place the fish on top. Do not stir.

3. Secure the lid on the pot. Close the pressure-release valve. Select MANUAL and set the pot at HIGH pressure for 1 minute. At the end of the cooking time, allow the pot to sit undisturbed for 5 minutes, then release any remaining pressure. Gently break the fish into large chunks and stir the soup.

4. Drizzle with the remaining 1 tablespoon sesame oil. Add sriracha and/or green onions, if desired, and serve.

PER SERVING

Calories: 190
Total Fat: 9g
Saturated Fat: 2g
Sodium: 480mg
Carbohydrates: 4g
Fiber: 1g
Sugars: 1g
Protein: 24g

FISH AND CORN CHOWDER

To make this faster, you can use a small can of creamed corn rather than puréeing the corn. Be sure to cut the potatoes into 1-inch cubes so they cook in the same time as the fish.

ACTIVE TIME	FUNCTION	RELEASE	TOTAL TIME
10 minutes	Manual (High)	Quick	25 minutes

Egg-Free · Nut-Free · Gluten-Free · Soy-Free · 30 Minutes or Less · SERVES 4

2 cups corn kernels (fresh or frozen, thawed), divided

1 pound frozen nonoily white fish fillets, such as grouper, tilapia, or perch

2 cups water

1 cup diced onion

1 cup diced (1 inch) long white potatoes

1 teaspoon kosher salt

1 teaspoon black pepper

½ teaspoon garlic powder

1 (5-ounce) can evaporated milk

Tabasco or other hot sauce, to taste

¼ cup chopped chives (optional)

1. In a blender, pulse 1 cup of the corn until you have a coarse purée.

2. In the Instant Pot, combine the fish, water, corn purée, remaining 1 cup corn kernels, onion, potatoes, salt, pepper, and garlic powder.

3. Secure the lid on the pot. Close the pressure-release valve. Select MANUAL and set the pot at HIGH pressure for 2 minutes. At the end of the cooking time, use a quick release to depressurize. Gently break the fish into large chunks.

4. Stir in the evaporated milk, Tabasco sauce to taste, and chives, if using, and serve.

PER SERVING

Calories: 290
Total Fat: 7g
Saturated Fat: 4g
Sodium: 610mg
Carbohydrates: 31g
Fiber: 3g
Sugars: 10g
Protein: 30g

FISH AND POTATO SOUP WITH SOUR CREAM AND DILL

Inspired by a Russian *ukha* soup, I love the combination of the clear broth, the root vegetables, and the creamy dill flavors added at the end. I like to leave the fish in large chunks and then cut them up before serving. This keeps the fish from overcooking.

ACTIVE TIME	FUNCTION	RELEASE	TOTAL TIME
10 minutes	Manual (High)	Quick	25 minutes

Egg-Free • Nut-Free • Gluten-Free • Grain-Free • Soy-Free • Low-Carb • 30 Minutes or Less • SERVES 4

1 pound frozen firm white fish fillets, such as cod, tilapia, or haddock

3 cups water

2 cups chopped red potatoes

1 cup diced onion

1 cup chopped carrots

1 teaspoon kosher salt

½ teaspoon black pepper

3 bay leaves

¼ cup sour cream

¼ cup chopped fresh dill

1. In the Instant Pot, combine the fish, water, potatoes, onion, carrots, salt, pepper, and bay leaves.

2. Secure the lid on the pot. Close the pressure-release valve. Select MANUAL and set the pot at HIGH pressure for 2 minutes. At the end of the cooking time, use a quick release to depressurize. Gently break the fish into large chunks.

3. Place the sour cream in a small bowl and slowly stir in a ladleful of hot broth to temper it. Pour this mixture into the soup. Discard the bay leaves, stir in the dill, and serve.

PER SERVING

Calories: 200
Total Fat: 4g
Saturated Fat: 2g
Sodium: 570mg
Carbohydrates: 20g
Fiber: 3g
Sugars: 4g
Protein: 23g

HONEY-MUSTARD SALMON WITH RICE AND VEGETABLES

Three things to know about this recipe: First, the sauce will look weird after cooking. But it blends together beautifully with a stir. Second, the rice may brown a little at the bottom, but it won't burn if you follow the directions exactly as written. Third, all of this is super-tasty!

ACTIVE TIME	FUNCTION	RELEASE	TOTAL TIME
10 minutes	Manual (High)	Natural/Quick	35 minutes

Egg-Free • Nut-Free • Dairy-Free • SERVES 4

1 cup long-grain basmati rice, rinsed and drained

1 cup diced onion

1 tablespoon vegetable oil

1 teaspoon kosher salt

1¼ cups water

1½ cups frozen peas and carrots

2 tablespoons Dijon mustard

1 tablespoon reduced-sodium soy sauce

1 tablespoon honey

2 cloves garlic, minced

½ teaspoon kosher salt

1 pound frozen skinless salmon fillets

1. In the Instant Pot, combine the rice, onion, oil, salt, and water. Scatter the peas and carrots on the top. Do not stir.

2. In a small bowl, whisk together the mustard, soy sauce, honey, garlic, and salt. Place the fillets in a 6×3- or 7×2-inch round heatproof pan. Pour the sauce over the fillets.

3. Place a trivet in the pot. Set the pan on the trivet.

4. Secure the lid on the pot. Close the pressure-release valve. Select MANUAL and set the pot at HIGH pressure for 4 minutes. At the end of the cooking time, allow the pot to sit undisturbed for 10 minutes, then release any remaining pressure.

5. Open the lid and remove the pan. Using a fork or whisk, blend the sauce until smooth. Stir the rice mixture, divide among the four plates, and place the salmon on top.

6. Drizzle the salmon and rice with the sauce and serve.

PER SERVING

Calories: 410
Total Fat: 11g
Saturated Fat: 2g

Sodium: 1,100mg
Carbohydrates: 49g
Fiber: 4g

Sugars: 6g
Protein: 28g

PAPRIKA-SPICED FISH AND VEGETABLE SOUP

Based on a Brazilian *moqueca*, I added tomatoes and a little extra paprika to give this light but filling soup some color and a slightly smoky taste. When combined with the creaminess of the coconut milk, it yields a colorful and comforting soup. Cut the vegetables in large chunks so they don't disintegrate into the soup.

ACTIVE TIME	FUNCTION	RELEASE	TOTAL TIME
15 minutes	Sauté (Normal); Manual (High)	Natural/Quick	30 minutes

Egg-Free · Nut-Free · Dairy-Free · Gluten-Free · Grain-Free · Soy-Free · Low-Carb · 30 Minutes or Less · SERVES 4

2 tablespoons coconut oil

4 large cloves garlic, minced

2 teaspoons smoked paprika

2 cups stemmed, seeded, and roughly chopped green bell peppers

2 cups sliced green onions

2 cups coarsely chopped tomatoes

1 cup coarsely chopped onion

½ cup chopped fresh cilantro

1 teaspoon kosher salt

1 pound frozen firm white fish fillets such as cod, tilapia, or haddock

1 cup water

½ cup full-fat coconut milk

2 tablespoons fresh lemon juice

1. Select SAUTÉ/Normal on the Instant Pot. When the pot is hot, add the coconut oil. Once the oil is hot, add the garlic and paprika, and let sizzle for about 5 seconds. Stir in the bell peppers, green onions, tomatoes, onion, cilantro, and salt. Add the fish and water.

2. Secure the lid on the pot. Close the pressure-release valve. Select MANUAL and set the pot at HIGH pressure for 1 minute. At the end of the cooking time, allow the pot to sit undisturbed for 5 minutes, then release any remaining pressure. Gently break the fish into large chunks.

3. Stir in the coconut milk and lemon juice and serve.

PER SERVING

Calories: 280
Total Fat: 14g
Saturated Fat: 11g
Sodium: 560mg
Carbohydrates: 17g
Fiber: 5g
Sugars: 7g
Protein: 24g

SALMON AND POTATO CURRY

I like to soak the frozen peas in hot water while this dish cooks. Then they are ready to stir in at the end of cooking. The pea-haters among you can choose to either omit, use corn, or use any other cooked or steamed vegetable you love. You can serve this with rice or naan or just eat it like a soup.

ACTIVE TIME	FUNCTION	RELEASE	TOTAL TIME
15 minutes	Manual (High)	Natural/Quick	30 minutes

Egg-Free • Nut-Free • Dairy-Free • Gluten-Free • Grain-Free • Soy-Free • Low-Carb • 30 Minutes or Less • SERVES 4

2 cups chopped long white potatoes

1 cup cherry tomatoes

½ cup diced onion

1 tablespoon minced fresh ginger

3 cloves garlic, minced

1 teaspoon ground turmeric

1 teaspoon kosher salt

1 teaspoon Garam Masala (page 221)

½ to 1 teaspoon cayenne pepper

½ cup water

1 (8-ounce) frozen salmon fillet

1 cup frozen peas, thawed

¾ cup full-fat coconut milk

½ cup chopped fresh cilantro

1. In the Instant Pot, combine the potatoes, tomatoes, onion, ginger, garlic, turmeric, salt, Garam Masala, cayenne, and water. Stir well. Lay the fillet on top of the vegetables.

2. Secure the lid on the pot. Close the pressure-release valve. Select MANUAL and set the pot at HIGH pressure for 1 minute. At the end of the cooking time, allow the pot to sit undisturbed for 5 minutes, then release any remaining pressure.

3. Gently break the fish into large chunks. Stir in the peas and coconut milk.

4. Garnish with cilantro and serve.

PER SERVING

Calories: 270
Total Fat: 13g
Saturated Fat: 9g
Sodium: 540mg
Carbohydrates: 23g
Fiber: 5g
Sugars: 4g
Protein: 16g

SALMON AND QUINOA SALAD

This is a great all-in-one meal, and it tastes fantastic when cold, which makes it perfect to take to lunch the next day. The peanuts add a lovely crunch to this salad, along with the fresh onions and cabbage. You can use any firm white fish for this recipe if you prefer.

ACTIVE TIME	FUNCTION	RELEASE	TOTAL TIME
15 minutes	Manual (High)	Natural/Quick	30 minutes

Egg-Free · Nut-Free · Dairy-Free · Soy-Free · Gluten-Free · 30 Minutes or Less · SERVES 4

For the Quinoa

1 cup quinoa, rinsed and drained

1 tablespoon extra-virgin olive oil

1 teaspoon kosher salt

1 cup frozen corn

1 (8-ounce) frozen skinless salmon fillet, thawed

For the Vinaigrette

¼ cup fresh lime juice

¼ cup extra-virgin olive oil

¼ cup chopped fresh cilantro

1 serrano pepper, seeded if desired, coarsely chopped

1 teaspoon kosher salt

For Finishing

1 cup finely shredded cabbage

1 cup shredded carrots

½ cup finely chopped fresh cilantro

2 tablespoons coarsely chopped roasted peanuts or nut of choice

¼ cup diced red onion

1. **For the Quinoa:** In the Instant Pot, combine the quinoa, olive oil, salt, and 1 cup of water. Scatter the corn on top.

2. Place a trivet in the pot. Set the fillet on the trivet.

3. Secure the lid on the pot. Close the pressure-release valve. Select MANUAL and set the pot at HIGH pressure for 1 minute. At the end of the cooking time, allow the pot to sit undisturbed for 5 minutes, then release any remaining pressure.

4. **For the Vinaigrette:** In a blender, combine the lime juice, olive oil, cilantro, serrano, and salt. Blend until smooth.

5. Carefully remove the fillet from the pot and break into large pieces.

6. **For Finishing:** In a large serving bowl, combine the salmon, quinoa mixture, cabbage, carrots, cilantro, peanuts, and onion. Toss with the vinaigrette and serve.

PER SERVING		
Calories: 490	Sodium: 530mg	Sugars: 5g
Total Fat: 27g	Carbohydrates: 42g	Protein: 21g
Saturated Fat: 4g	Fiber: 13g	

LENTILS, BEANS, AND LEGUMES

HOW TO COOK BEANS IN THE INSTANT POT

Before we start to talk about how to cook these, there are a few terms we should get straight.

Beans, lentils, legumes, pulses, dal . . . what do all these terms mean?

Legumes are plants whose fruit are enclosed in a pod. There are more than 13,000 varieties, and these include things like fresh soybeans, peanuts, fresh beans, etc.

Pulses are dried seeds of legumes. So, all pulses are legumes, but not all legumes are pulses. Examples include chickpeas, dried soybeans, mung beans, and kidney beans.

Dal is a ubiquitous term that is used to describe beans and lentils and often split lentils or split beans.

One Bean, Four Lives

Most beans can be used in one of four ways: whole, split with skin, split but without skin, and ground. As a cook, this is important because it affects cooking times.

As a rule of thumb for pressure cookers, whole beans take 30 minutes, split beans (such as split peas, red lentils, etc.) take between three to ten minutes, and ground beans, of course, are used in batter such as chickpea flour.

What this means is that you can choose to substitute whole beans for other whole beans in these recipes if you are looking to experiment. Substituting pinto beans for kidney beans will work without any changes to cooking times. But if you substitute red kidney beans (30 minutes) for red lentils (3 minutes), your results will be terrible.

What Are Heirloom Beans and Do I Need Them?

Heirloom basically means that those beans are genetically different in that they haven't been crossbred with any other varietal or species of beans. Do you need them? I find them to be slightly fuller flavored, but the best part is that they're often variegated, speckled, and just pretty looking. But they all cook up the same.

▲ Cannellini

▲ French Lentils

▲ Black-Eyed Peas

▸ 16-Bean Blend

◂ Pinto Beans

▲ Adzuki Beans

▲ Pardina Lentils

◂ Navy Beans

◂ Mung Beans

▲ Lima Beans

▲ Chickpeas

The variety is intriguing and fun, but no, you don't have to use heirloom beans to find nutritious, good-for-you sources of protein and fiber.

Do I Have to Soak Beans for Pressure Cooking?

This is a question with no clear answer. Some people do, and others don't. I do a hybrid method and I will explain why. Note that you never need to soak split beans such as red or yellow lentils and split peas.

All the recipes in this book were tested with beans soaked in very hot water for one hour. This is why I do this. If I write a recipe for kidney beans to cook for thirty minutes, and you use beans that are very, very old, it will take longer than thirty minutes. Then you will think I gave you a bad recipe, and worse, dinner will be late.

I don't know about you, but most days I can barely remember how old I am, let alone how old the beans in my pantry are. I also don't know if they arrived in my pantry as old beans or young beans.

I find it best to soak whole beans. In your cooking you can prepare beans in one of five ways. I have listed them in order of prettiest resultant beans and most even cooking to—well, they're cooked but they're not pretty. Note also longer soak times lead to a better breakdown in the indigestible sugars in the bean, so it's easier on your stomach as well.

Various Ways to Soak Beans for the Instant Pot

1. **Overnight:** Soak 1 cup of beans in about 3 to 4 cups of water overnight. Drain the beans and use as directed. After 8 hours, place the beans in the refrigerator, otherwise you'll be dealing with semifermented beans.

2. **Overnight-freezer method:** This isn't really a different method but rather a clever hack my husband, Roger, suggested that worked really well. When you're soaking overnight as listed above, soak twice as many beans as the recipe calls for. In the morning, put half the soaked beans into a zip-top bag and place the bag in the freezer. I found that with this method, I didn't even have to defrost the beans, I just threw in the frozen beans and cooked the recipes as written. I love this sort of #ruthlessefficiency, don't you?

3. **Hot-water method:** Soak 1 cup of beans in about 3 to 4 cups of very hot water (preferably boiling water) for an hour. The beans will have plumped and absorbed most of the water in this time. Drain the beans and use as directed. This is what I did for all the bean recipes in this book. The beans cook consistently with very little breaking. This is my preferred last-minute method.

4. **Pressure-cooker soaking:** Place 1 cup of beans and 3 to 4 cups of water in the Instant Pot. Close the lid. Press PRESSURE COOK on HIGH for 0 minutes (yes, 0 minutes, that's a thing). Allow the pot to rest undisturbed for 15 minutes. Then, release all remaining pressure. Drain the beans and use as directed. This method is very much like the hot-water method—you're just using the pressure cooker to heat the water for you to some extent. Note that beans are more likely to burst open with this method of soaking, so you could be trading beauty for convenience here.

5. **Don't soak:** That's right, be a maverick! In this case, I suggest you add 5 to 10 minutes to the cooking time under pressure. You may need to add a little more water as well. Note that this may adversely impact the other ingredients in the recipe. It is also more likely to cause gastric distress for people, and your beans will be more likely to split and not be pretty beans. I suggest you do this only once you're really comfortable working with different types of beans. For what it's worth, I never cook them this way. But your mileage may vary and this may well be your favorite method.

Should I Salt the Beans While Soaking?

Salting the beans, especially if you plan to use the pressure cooker soaking method, helps to keep the beans from splitting. I do not salt my beans as I try to eat less salt as a rule, and then when I'm cooking a dish, it's hard for me to estimate how much salt to add. You can choose to add salt to the soaking water if you wish.

Keep in mind that all these recipes ask you to add salt for cooking anyway, which I think lends a lovely flavor to the beans.

How Long Do I Cook Beans in the Instant Pot?

There are many charts available on how long to cook various beans, but here's the rule of thumb I start with:

- Split legumes or smaller lentils such as split green peas, split garbanzo beans, black lentils, brown lentils, etc., are in the 2-to-5-minutes camp. Of these, split garbanzos (*chana dal*) should be cooked up to 10 minutes if you want them to disintegrate into the dish.
- Smaller beans such as black-eyed peas, navy beans, and green whole mung beans should be cooked for 10 minutes under pressure.

- Large whole beans such as black beans, kidney beans, pinto beans, etc., should be cooked for 30 to 40 minutes. If you want tender but whole beans, 30 minutes will work. For beans that need to cook down into the soup, you may want to do 40 or even 50 minutes.

What this means is that you can mix and match beans at least with respect to cooking times.

- Any split dal recipe will work with another.
- Any small bean recipe will work with another.
- Any whole bean recipe will work with another.

Feel free to experiment on a day when you're not rushing around trying to get dinner on the table quickly. It's always easy to recook under-cooked beans, so start on the lower end of the scale and add time as needed.

Beans in Pounds, Cups, and Cans

- Usually a 1-lb bag of beans equates to about 2½ to 3 cups of dried beans. This will, of course, depend on how big or small the beans are, but that's a good rule of thumb to start with.
- A 15-oz can is about 1½ cups of cooked beans or about ¾ cup of dried beans.
- Beans will double or triple in volume when cooked, so 1 cup of dried beans will yield almost 3 cups of cooked beans. Smaller beans like black-eyed peas tend to double, but chickpeas, for example, tend to triple, so 1 cup of dried beans will yield about 2 cups of cooked black-eyed peas but closer to 3 cups of cooked chickpeas.
- Because beans will double or triple in volume once cooked, be careful not to overfill your Instant Pot.

THREE-INGREDIENT TOMATO LENTILS

This crazy, utterly ludicrous, totally #ruthlesslyefficient, and ultimately surprisingly authentic-tasting Indian dal recipe is quite typical of my cooking style. Minimal ingredients, maximum flavor. So now you have no excuse to not eat healthy. Normally, you'd use onions, garlic, ginger, oil, cumin, etc. But no. We won't be doing that here. You can use fresh tomatoes and chiles if you prefer. Whatever you do, do *not* use the hot version of the diced tomatoes and green chiles. I tried that, and even doubling the dal after that didn't help to make it more edible!

ACTIVE TIME	FUNCTION	RELEASE	TOTAL TIME
5 minutes	Manual (High)	Natural/Quick	55 minutes

Egg-Free • Nut-Free • Dairy-Free • Gluten-Free • Grain-Free • Soy-Free • Vegan •
SERVES 6 as a main dish

1 (10-ounce) can diced tomatoes and green chiles (mild or original)

1 cup chana dal (split yellow pigeon peas) or split dried chickpeas

2½ cups water

1½ teaspoons kosher salt

1 teaspoon ground turmeric

Rice, naan, or tortillas (optional)

1. In the Instant Pot, combine the diced tomatoes and green chiles, chana dal, water, salt, and turmeric.

2. Secure the lid on the pot. Close the pressure-release valve. Select MANUAL and set the pot at HIGH pressure for 30 minutes. At the end of the cooking time, allow the pot to sit undisturbed for 10 minutes, then release any remaining pressure.

3. Serve with rice, naan, or tortillas, if desired.

PER SERVING

Calories: 120
Total Fat: 1g
Saturated Fat: 0g
Sodium: 680mg
Carbohydrates: 23g
Fiber: 6g
Sugars: 0g
Protein: 8g

BLACK BEAN AND CHORIZO STEW

Hearty, spicy, and very little chop and prep. I used turkey chorizo to lower the fat, but you can use regular chorizo. Be sure to use the Mexican chorizo (fresh sausage in casing) and not smoked Spanish chorizo. Also, be sure not to use the hot version of the diced tomatoes and green chiles for this, unless you want to blow the roof of your mouth off!

ACTIVE TIME	FUNCTION	RELEASE	TOTAL TIME
15 minutes	Sauté (Normal); Manual (High)	Natural/Quick	1 hour 15 minutes plus 1 hour soaking time

Egg-Free · Nut-Free · Dairy-Free · Gluten-Free · Grain-Free · Soy-Free · SERVES 6 as a main dish

1 cup dried black beans

1 cup diced onion

1 cup stemmed, seeded, and roughly chopped bell pepper (any color and/ or mixed)

8 ounces ground turkey chorizo

3 cloves garlic, minced

1 (10-ounce) can diced tomatoes and green chiles (mild or original)

1½ cups water

½ cup chopped fresh cilantro

1 tablespoon ground cumin

1½ teaspoons kosher salt

Optional toppings:
chopped fresh cilantro, crumbled queso fresco, sliced pickled jalapeños

1. One hour before you plan to cook, place the dried beans in a bowl and cover with hot water by 2 inches; drain before using.

2. Select SAUTÉ/Normal on the Instant Pot. When the pot is hot, add the onion, bell pepper, chorizo, and garlic. Break up the chorizo with a wooden spoon. Add the tomatoes and chiles, beans, water, cilantro, cumin, and salt.

3. Secure the lid on the pot. Close the pressure-release valve. Select MANUAL and set the pot at HIGH pressure for 40 minutes. At the end of the cooking time, allow the pot to sit undisturbed for 10 minutes, then release any remaining pressure.

4. Using an immersion blender or the back of a spoon, roughly purée some of the soup to thicken, mashing about half the beans. Add additional water if needed.

5. Serve with optional toppings, if desired.

PER SERVING

Calories: 200	Sodium: 840mg	Sugars: 2g
Total Fat: 5g	Carbohydrates: 26g	Protein: 13g
Saturated Fat: 1g	Fiber: 6g	

BLACK-EYED PEAS WITH TOMATOES AND GREENS

Black-eyed peas cook so fast in a pressure cooker that I often make them on days when I need something fast. This, plus some rice or cornbread, and you've got yourself a good old-fashioned and delicious Southern meal. Feel free to stir in some ham at the end if you want.

ACTIVE TIME	FUNCTION	RELEASE	TOTAL TIME
10 minutes	Manual (High)	Natural/Quick	45 minutes plus 1 hour soaking time

Egg-Free · Nut-Free · Dairy-Free · Gluten-Free · Grain-Free · Soy-Free · Vegan ·
SERVES 6 as a main dish

1 cup dried black-eyed peas

1 (14.5-ounce) can diced tomatoes or 1½ cups diced fresh tomatoes

1 cup diced onion

1 cup stemmed, seeded, and roughly chopped green bell pepper

1½ cups water

3 cloves garlic, minced

1½ teaspoons kosher salt

1 teaspoon dried thyme

½ teaspoon black pepper

2 cups baby spinach

2 tablespoons apple cider vinegar

1 tablespoon hot sauce, or to taste

1. One hour before you plan to cook, place the dried peas in a bowl and cover with hot water by 2 inches; drain before using.

2. In the Instant Pot, combine the tomatoes, drained black-eyed peas, onion, bell pepper, water, garlic, salt, thyme, and pepper.

3. Secure the lid on the pot. Close the pressure-release valve. Select MANUAL and set the pot at HIGH pressure for 15 minutes. At the end of the cooking time, allow the pot to sit undisturbed for 10 minutes, then release any remaining pressure.

4. Stir in the spinach, vinegar, and hot sauce and serve.

NOTE: You can make white rice pot-in-pot while you are making the beans. This is also good served with cornbread.

PER SERVING

Calories: 160	Sodium: 730mg	Sugars: 5g
Total Fat: 1g	Carbohydrates: 29g	Protein: 9g
Saturated Fat: 0g	Fiber: 8g	

CHICKPEA SALAD

I grew up eating this salad, mainly because my mom convinced me it was junk food, and what kid doesn't love junk food? She was a clever woman, and I still think of her every time I eat this. If you can get ahold of some chaat masala to sprinkle on this, you'll think you've died and gone to heaven. But even without it, it's a lovely and filling salad.

ACTIVE TIME	FUNCTION	RELEASE	TOTAL TIME
10 minutes	Manual (High)	Natural/Quick	55 minutes plus 2 hours soaking/chilling time

Egg-Free · Nut-Free · Dairy-Free · Gluten-Free · Grain-Free · Soy-Free · Vegan ·
SERVES 4 as a main dish

1 cup dried chickpeas

3 bay leaves

3 cups water

2 cups diced cucumbers

2 cups diced tomatoes

¾ cup red onion, finely minced

½ cup chopped fresh cilantro

¼ cup fresh lemon juice

½ teaspoon cayenne pepper, or to taste

1 teaspoon kosher salt

1. One hour before you plan to cook, place the dried chickpeas in a bowl and cover with hot water by 2 inches; drain before using.

2. In the Instant Pot, combine the chickpeas, bay leaves, and water.

3. Secure the lid on the pot. Close the pressure-release valve. Select MANUAL and set the pot at HIGH pressure for 25 minutes. At the end of the cooking time, allow the pot to sit undisturbed for 10 minutes, then release any remaining pressure. Drain the chickpeas and allow to cool slightly. Discard the bay leaves.

4. In a large bowl, combine the cucumbers, tomatoes, chickpeas, onion, cilantro, lemon juice, cayenne, and salt.

5. Chill for 1 to 2 hours before serving.

PER SERVING

Calories: 200
Total Fat: 3g
Saturated Fat: 0g

Sodium: 500mg
Carbohydrates: 36g
Fiber: 10g

Sugars: 10g
Protein: 11g

GARLICKY WHITE BEAN DIP

We were brainstorming on set as we shot my *Instant Pot Miracle Vegetarian* book, and our very talented food stylist, Monica Pieroni, suggested a garlicky bean dip. I think she forgot about it, but the idea intrigued me, since many other dip recipes start with canned beans. We can all thank her for inspiring me to create this!

ACTIVE TIME	FUNCTION	RELEASE	TOTAL TIME
15 minutes	Sauté (Normal); Manual (High)	Natural/Quick	50 minutes plus 1 hour soaking time

Egg-Free • Nut-Free • Dairy-Free • Gluten-Free • Grain-Free • Soy-Free • Vegan •
SERVES 6 as a side dish (makes 2 cups)

1 cup dried cannellini beans

2 tablespoons vegetable oil

¼ cup thinly sliced garlic cloves

1 cup water

1 teaspoon black pepper

2 bay leaves

½ cup fresh lemon juice

1 teaspoon kosher salt

Pita chips and/or raw vegetables, for dipping

PER SERVING
Calories: 150
Total Fat: 5g
Saturated Fat: 1g
Sodium: 330mg
Carbohydrates: 21g
Fiber: 5g
Sugars: 1g
Protein: 7g

1. One hour before you plan to cook, place the dried beans in a bowl and cover with hot water by 2 inches; drain before using.

2. Select SAUTÉ/Normal on the Instant Pot. When the pot is hot, add the oil. Once the oil is hot, add the garlic. Cook until the edges are browned, 5 to 8 minutes. Remove half the garlic and reserve for garnishing. Add the beans, water, pepper, and bay leaves.

3. Secure the lid on the pot. Close the pressure-release valve. Select MANUAL and set the pot at HIGH pressure for 15 minutes. At the end of the cooking time, allow the pot to sit undisturbed for 10 minutes, then release any remaining pressure. Discard the bay leaves. Drain the beans, reserving the water.

4. Add the lemon juice and salt. Using an immersion blender, purée the beans until smooth, adding small amounts of the reserved bean-cooking water to achieve the desired consistency.

5. Garnish with the fried garlic, and serve with pita chips or raw vegetables for dipping.

HARISSA BUTTERNUT AND CHICKPEA STEW

Make this harissa and use it on everything! I've used it in my air fryer cookbooks to flavor lamb chops and beef. It does a particularly good job in this stew, and it's a one-shot flavoring that adds so much. The butternut squash cooks down a bit into the soup and serves to make it that much tastier.

ACTIVE TIME	FUNCTION	RELEASE	TOTAL TIME
10 minutes	Manual (High)	Quick	1 hour 5 minutes plus 1 hour soaking time

Egg-Free · Nut-Free · Dairy-Free · Gluten-Free · Grain-Free · Soy-Free · Vegan ·
SERVES 4 as a main dish

1 cup dried chickpeas

1 cup diced onion

2 tablespoons tomato paste

2 tablespoons Harissa (page 222)

3 cloves garlic, minced

1½ teaspoons ground cumin

1½ teaspoons kosher salt

1 teaspoon black pepper

1½ cups water

1 (16-ounce) package diced butternut squash, fresh or frozen

2 tablespoons fresh lemon juice

4 to 6 fried eggs (optional)

PER SERVING

Calories: 270
Total Fat: 7g
Saturated Fat: 1g
Sodium: 820mg

Carbohydrates: 46g
Fiber: 11g
Sugars: 9g
Protein: 11g

1. One hour before you plan to cook, place the dried chickpeas in a bowl and cover with hot water by 2 inches; drain before using.

2. In the Instant Pot, combine the chickpeas, onion, tomato paste, Harissa, garlic, cumin, salt, pepper, and water.

3. Secure the lid on the pot. Close the pressure-release valve. Select MANUAL and set the pot at HIGH pressure for 35 minutes. At the end of the cooking time, use a quick release to depressurize. Add the squash. Secure the lid on the pot. Close the pressure-release valve. Select MANUAL and set the pot at HIGH pressure for 0 minutes. At the end of the cooking time, use a quick release to depressurize.

4. Open the lid, and stir the stew. The squash will disintegrate, making a thick purée.

5. To serve, stir in the lemon juice. Divide among serving bowls, and top with fried eggs, if using.

NOTE: If you would like to keep the butternut squash in whole chunks, you may choose to steam it in the microwave or on the stovetop until it is tender-crisp, and add it to the cooked chickpeas.

LENTIL AND TOMATO SALAD

I've made this with green lentils as well as these red ones. For green lentils, cook it for 6 minutes under pressure and then proceed as directed. This one tastes great cold as well—I eat it straight out of the fridge.

ACTIVE TIME	FUNCTION	RELEASE	TOTAL TIME
10 minutes	Manual (High)	Natural/Quick	35 minutes

Egg-Free · Nut-Free · Dairy-Free · Gluten-Free · Grain-Free · Soy-Free · Vegan · SERVES 6 as a main dish

1 cup dried red lentils

2½ teaspoons kosher salt, divided

2 bay leaves

3 cups water

⅓ cup apple cider vinegar

¼ cup vegetable oil

2 teaspoons ground cumin

1 teaspoon ground allspice

4 cups chopped fresh kale

½ cup chopped fresh parsley

2 cups chopped fresh tomatoes

Optional stir-ins:
crumbled feta cheese; cayenne pepper; chopped, cooked beets; chopped, cooked potatoes; cooked black beans

1. In the Instant Pot, combine the lentils, 1½ teaspoons of the salt, bay leaves, and water.

2. Secure the lid on the pot. Close the pressure-release valve. Select MANUAL and set the pot at HIGH pressure for 0 minutes. At the end of the cooking time, allow the pot to sit undisturbed for 5 minutes, then release any remaining pressure. Drain the lentils, rinse under cold water, and set aside to cool for 15 minutes. Discard the bay leaves.

3. Meanwhile, in a large bowl, whisk together the vinegar, oil, cumin, allspice, and the remaining 1 teaspoon salt. Add the kale and parsley, and, using your hands, massage the kale. (This will help soften the kale, reduce some of the bitterness, and allow the seasonings to penetrate.)

4. Add the lentils and tomatoes, as well as any desired stir-ins, and serve.

PER SERVING

Calories: 210
Total Fat: 10g
Saturated Fat: 1g
Sodium: 1,130mg
Carbohydrates: 24g
Fiber: 5g
Sugars: 2g
Protein: 9g

MIXED BEAN SALAD

Here's another recipe I used to make twenty-plus years ago, especially during hot Texas summers. I like this method of making the beans from either the French haricot vert–style thin beans or French-cut green beans.

ACTIVE TIME	FUNCTION	RELEASE	TOTAL TIME
10 minutes	Manual (High)	Natural/Quick	1 hour plus 1 hour chilling time

Egg-Free • Nut-Free • Dairy-Free • Gluten-Free • Grain-Free • Soy-Free • Vegan •
SERVES 6 as a side dish

For the Salad

½ cup dried kidney beans

½ cup dried pinto beans

4 cups water

3 bay leaves

2 cups frozen French-cut green beans

For the Vinaigrette

⅓ cup vegetable oil

¼ cup apple cider vinegar

3 tablespoons prepared yellow mustard

2 teaspoons sugar (optional)

1 teaspoon kosher salt

1 teaspoon black pepper

Optional stir-ins:

cooked corn, diced red onion, diced bell pepper (any color or mixed), diced cucumber, diced tomato, diced avocado, chopped fresh cilantro, chopped fresh parsley, minced jalapeño

1. **For the Salad:** One hour before you plan to cook, place the dried kidney beans and pinto beans in a bowl and cover with hot water by 2 inches; drain before using.

2. In the Instant Pot, combine the kidney and pinto beans, water, and bay leaves.

3. Secure the lid on the pot. Close the pressure-release valve. Select MANUAL and set the pot at HIGH pressure for 20 minutes. At the end of the cooking time, allow the pot to sit undisturbed for 10 minutes, then release any remaining pressure.

4. Open the lid, and stir in the green beans. Close the lid and allow the green beans to cook in the residual heat for about 10 minutes. Drain the beans and allow to cool. Discard the bay leaves.

5. **For the Vinaigrette:** In a large bowl, whisk together the oil, vinegar, mustard, sugar (if using), salt, and pepper.

6. Add the beans and desired stir-ins. Toss gently to mix.

7. Chill for 1 to 2 hours before serving.

PER SERVING

Calories: 220
Total Fat: 13g
Saturated Fat: 2g

Sodium: 410mg
Carbohydrates: 20g
Fiber: 7g

Sugars: 2g
Protein: 7g

MUNG BEANS WITH TURNIP GREENS

Most people think of mung bean sprouts when they think of mung beans, but the beans themselves are a powerhouse of both nutrition and flavor. The turnip greens add a little mustardy bitterness to the soup, which a lot of people love. If that's not your thing, just stir in spinach or Swiss chard after the beans are cooked.

ACTIVE TIME	FUNCTION	RELEASE	TOTAL TIME
10 minutes	Manual (High)	Natural/Quick	45 minutes

Egg-Free · Nut-Free · Dairy-Free · Gluten-Free · Grain-Free · Soy-Free · Vegan · Low-Carb · SERVES 6 as a main dish

1 cup dried green mung beans

1 cup diced onion

2 cups diced tomatoes, divided

3 cloves garlic, minced

1 tablespoon minced fresh ginger

2 teaspoons Garam Masala (page 221)

2 teaspoons kosher salt

½ teaspoon black pepper

1 teaspoon cayenne pepper

2 cups water

1 (14-ounce) package frozen turnip greens with diced turnips

3 tablespoons fresh lemon juice

1. In the Instant Pot, combine the mung beans, onion, 1 cup of the tomatoes, garlic, ginger, Garam Masala, salt, pepper, cayenne, and water. Stir well. Place the greens and turnips on top. Do not stir.

2. Secure the lid on the pot. Close the pressure-release valve. Select MANUAL and set the pot at HIGH pressure for 15 minutes. At the end of the cooking time, allow the pot to sit undisturbed for 10 minutes, then release any remaining pressure.

3. Stir in the remaining 1 cup tomatoes and lemon juice and serve.

PER SERVING

Calories: 170
Total Fat: 1g
Saturated Fat: 0g
Sodium: 680mg
Carbohydrates: 30g
Fiber: 8g
Sugars: 6g
Protein: 10g

PASTA FAGIOLI SOUP

I lightened this by using half the meat and half the pasta that typical recipes called for. I highly recommend fresh spinach for this recipe. You can use cooked or canned kidney beans. I have stayed away from that in other recipes, but in this case, it seemed easier to use cooked beans so that you could cook everything at the same time. I find it useful to make twice the beans I need for a recipe and then freeze half for such a use.

ACTIVE TIME	FUNCTION	RELEASE	TOTAL TIME
10 minutes	Sauté (Normal); Manual (High)	Natural/Quick	30 minutes

Egg-Free • Nut-Free • Dairy-Free • Soy-Free • 30 Minutes or Less • SERVES 4 as a main dish

1 tablespoon vegetable oil

8 ounces (90% lean) ground beef

2 cups diced onion

3 cloves garlic, minced

1 (14.5-ounce) can diced tomatoes, or 2 cups diced fresh tomatoes

4 tablespoons tomato paste

1 tablespoon Italian seasoning

1 Kosher salt and black pepper

3 cups water, plus more if desired

1 (14.5-ounce) can kidney beans, rinsed and drained (1½ cups cooked)

½ cup small elbow macaroni

4 cups chopped baby spinach

½ cup chopped fresh parsley

2 teaspoons hot sauce (optional)

½ cup shredded Parmesan cheese (optional)

Breadsticks or crusty baguette (optional)

1. Select SAUTÉ/Normal on the Instant Pot. When the pot is hot, add the oil. Once the oil is hot, add the ground beef and break it up with a wooden spoon.

2. Add the onion and garlic and stir. Add the tomatoes, tomato paste, Italian seasoning, 1 teaspoon each salt and pepper, and water.

3. Stir well to dissolve the tomato paste. Add the beans, macaroni, and spinach.

4. Secure the lid on the pot. Close the pressure-release valve. Select MANUAL and set the pot at HIGH pressure for 4 minutes. At the end of the cooking time, allow the pot to sit undisturbed for 5 minutes, then release any remaining pressure. Add additional water if you want a thinner soup.

5. Stir in the parsley. Add the hot sauce and sprinkle with Parmesan, if using. Serve with breadsticks, if desired.

PER SERVING		
Calories: 310	Sodium: 1,020mg	Sugars: 8g
Total Fat: 9g	Carbohydrates: 37g	Protein: 20g
Saturated Fat: 3g	Fiber: 8g	

RED LENTIL SOUP WITH HARISSA

Here's another reason to make your own harissa from the recipe I've provided (page 222). This hearty soup benefits from the harissa during cooking as well as the last-minute burst of flavor from the fresh harissa at the end. I usually serve this as soup the first day. Leftovers get a little zap of chopped cilantro and are served over rice as a rice-and-dal variation the next day.

ACTIVE TIME	FUNCTION	RELEASE	TOTAL TIME
10 minutes	Manual (High)	Natural/Quick	40 minutes

Egg-Free · Nut-Free · Dairy-Free · Gluten-Free · Grain-Free · Soy-Free · Vegan ·
SERVES 6 as a side dish

1 cup split red lentils

1 cup diced onion

3 cloves garlic, minced

¼ cup Harissa, divided (page 222)

1 teaspoon kosher salt

3½ cups water

2 tablespoons fresh lemon juice

PER SERVING

Calories: 170
Total Fat: 5g
Saturated Fat: 1g
Sodium: 400mg
Carbohydrates: 24g
Fiber: 4g
Sugars: 1g
Protein: 8g

1. In the Instant Pot, combine the lentils, onion, garlic, 2 tablespoons of the Harissa, salt, and water. Stir well.

2. Secure the lid on the pot. Close the pressure-release valve. Select MANUAL and set the pot at HIGH pressure for 8 minutes. At the end of the cooking time, allow the pot to sit undisturbed for 10 minutes, then release any remaining pressure.

3. Open the lid, and using an immersion blender, purée the soup until coarsely puréed.

4. Stir in the lemon juice and swirl in the remaining 2 tablespoons Harissa, leaving some red swirls showing in the soup.

VEGAN REFRIED BEANS

I've been making this recipe for years. Although I used to make it with bacon, I cooked it once for our vegetarian friends Sachin and Harsha, and we all loved them with coconut oil. It adds a hint of coconut flavor, which is very pleasing.

ACTIVE TIME	FUNCTION	RELEASE	TOTAL TIME
15 minutes	Manual (High)	Natural/Quick	1 hour 15 minutes plus 1 hour soaking time

Egg-Free • Nut-Free • Dairy-Free • Gluten-Free • Grain-Free • Soy-Free • Vegan •
SERVES 4 as a side dish

1 cup dried pinto beans

1 cup chopped onion

2½ cups water

1 jalapeño, chopped

4 large cloves garlic, minced

2 teaspoons ground cumin

1 teaspoon kosher salt

1 teaspoon dried oregano

2 bay leaves

¼ cup coconut oil

1 tablespoon Mexican red chili powder (not cayenne)

¼ cup chopped fresh cilantro

Sliced jalapeño (optional)

PER SERVING

Calories: 290
Total Fat: 14g
Saturated Fat: 12g
Sodium: 500mg
Carbohydrates: 32g
Fiber: 11g
Sugars: 4g
Protein: 10g

1. One hour before you plan to cook, place the dried beans in a bowl and cover with hot water by 2 inches; drain before using.

2. In the Instant Pot, combine the beans, onion, water, jalapeño, garlic, cumin, salt, oregano, and bay leaves.

3. Secure the lid on the pot. Close the pressure-release valve. Select MANUAL and set the pot at HIGH pressure for 35 minutes. At the end of the cooking time, allow the pot to sit undisturbed for 15 minutes, then release any remaining pressure.

4. Open the lid, and using the back of a spoon, mash some of the beans to thicken. Discard the bay leaves.

5. Heat a 12-inch frying pan over high heat. Add the coconut oil, and reduce heat to medium. Add the chili powder, and sauté, taking care not to burn the spice, 10 to 15 seconds.

6. Add the mashed beans a little at a time. (You may need to add some water to get a looser texture.)

7. Garnish with cilantro and jalapeño, if using, and serve.

SIMPLE PINTO BEAN STEW

I judge a Mexican restaurant by their salsa (they must have spicy salsa on their secret menu) and by their pinto beans. This is a super-simple dish, but it has amazing flavor without one ingredient overpowering another.

ACTIVE TIME	FUNCTION	RELEASE	TOTAL TIME
10 minutes	Manual (High)	Natural/Quick	1 hour plus 1 hour soaking time

Egg-Free · Nut-Free · Dairy-Free · Gluten-Free · Grain-Free · Soy-Free · Vegan · SERVES 4 as a main dish

1 cup dried pinto beans

1 cup diced onion

2 cups water

¾ cup chopped fresh cilantro, divided

4 slices bacon, diced (optional, see Note)

4 to 6 cloves garlic, thinly sliced

½ to 1 serrano pepper, seeded if desired, diced

2 teaspoons dried oregano

1½ teaspoons kosher salt

1 tablespoon fresh lime juice

PER SERVING

Calories: 170
Total Fat: 0g
Saturated Fat: 0g
Sodium: 720mg
Carbohydrates: 32g
Fiber: 11g
Sugars: 4g
Protein: 10g

1. One hour before you plan to cook, place the dried beans in a bowl and cover with hot water by 2 inches; drain before using.

2. In the Instant Pot, combine the beans, onion, water, ½ cup of the cilantro, bacon (if using), garlic, serrano, oregano, and salt.

3. Secure the lid on the pot. Close the pressure-release valve. Select MANUAL and set the pot at HIGH pressure for 30 minutes. At the end of the cooking time, allow the pot to sit undisturbed for 10 minutes, then release any remaining pressure.

4. Open the lid, and using the back of a spoon, mash some of the beans to thicken.

5. Stir in the lime juice and the remaining ¼ cup cilantro and serve.

NOTE: To make the dish vegan, omit the bacon.

WHITE BEAN CHILI

In this case, it's not the chili that's white as much as it is the beans. The evaporated milk is optional but makes for a lovely finish to this chili.

ACTIVE TIME	FUNCTION	RELEASE	TOTAL TIME
15 minutes	Manual (High)	Natural/Quick	1 hour 5 minutes plus 1 hour soaking time

Egg-Free • Nut-Free • Dairy-Free • Gluten-Free • Soy-Free • Vegan • SERVES 4 as a main dish

1 cup dried great northern beans

1 cup diced onion

2 cups water

3 cloves garlic, minced

1 tablespoon chili powder

2 teaspoons dried oregano

1½ teaspoons kosher salt

2 cups corn kernels (fresh or frozen, thawed)

1 (5-ounce) can evaporated milk, or ½ cup cashew cream (optional, see Note)

2 tablespoons fresh lime juice

½ cup chopped fresh cilantro

1. One hour before you plan to cook, place the dried beans in a bowl and cover with hot water by 2 inches; drain before using.

2. In the Instant Pot, combine the beans, onion, water, garlic, chili powder, oregano, and salt.

3. Secure the lid on the pot. Close the pressure-release valve. Select MANUAL and set the pot at HIGH pressure for 30 minutes. At the end of the cooking time, allow the pot to sit undisturbed for 10 minutes, then release any remaining pressure.

4. Stir in corn the and evaporated milk, if desired. Close the lid and allow the corn to cook in the residual heat, 2 to 3 minutes.

5. Stir in the lime juice and cilantro and serve.

NOTE: To make cashew cream, place ½ cup cashews in a small bowl with cool water to cover. Let soak 4 hours; drain. Place in a blender with ¼ cup fresh water and blend until smooth.

PER SERVING

Calories: 290
Total Fat: 5g
Saturated Fat: 2g
Sodium: 840mg
Carbohydrates: 52g
Fiber: 12g
Sugars: 11g
Protein: 16g

YELLOW SPLIT PEAS WITH SPINACH

This dal is nutritious and easy, but it's also very pretty. Serve it with naan or rice—or even freshly baked bread with lots of butter.

ACTIVE TIME	FUNCTION	RELEASE	TOTAL TIME
15 minutes	Sauté (Normal); Manual (High)	Natural/Quick	45 minutes

Egg-Free • Nut-Free • Dairy-Free • Gluten-Free • Grain-Free • Soy-Free • Vegan •
SERVES 4 as a main dish

2 tablespoons vegetable oil or ghee

2 teaspoons cumin seeds

1 cup diced onion

1 cup diced tomatoes

3 cloves garlic, minced

1 tablespoon minced fresh ginger

1 teaspoon ground turmeric

1 teaspoon ground cumin

1 teaspoon kosher salt

½ teaspoon cayenne pepper

1 cup yellow split peas

2 cups water

1 (8-ounce) package chopped frozen spinach

¼ cup chopped fresh cilantro or parsley

1. Select SAUTÉ/Normal on the Instant Pot. When the pot is hot, add the oil. Once the oil is hot, add the cumin seeds and let sputter and sizzle for 15 seconds. Add the onion, tomatoes, garlic, and ginger. Stir to combine. Add the turmeric, cumin, salt, and cayenne and cook, stirring constantly, about 30 seconds.

2. Add the split peas and water. Stir to combine. Place the spinach on top. Do not stir.

3. Secure the lid on the pot. Close the pressure-release valve. Select MANUAL and set the pot at HIGH pressure for 10 minutes. At the end of the cooking time, allow the pot to sit undisturbed for 10 minutes, then release any remaining pressure.

4. Stir to combine. Garnish with cilantro and serve.

PER SERVING

Calories: 270
Total Fat: 8g
Saturated Fat: 1g
Sodium: 530mg
Carbohydrates: 38g
Fiber: 17g
Sugars: 4g
Protein: 13g

RICE AND GRAINS

PERFECT PRESSURE-COOKER RICE

Rice is probably the most commonly cooked food all over the world, and yet many of us still struggle to cook the perfect pot of it. I will share what I have learned through research and lots of trial and error to help you cook the perfect rice in the Instant Pot.

To do that, it is important to first understand the different types of rice, their distinguishing characteristics, and best uses for each type.

How to Think About Rice

Rice has two types of starches.

- There's amylopectin, which makes the rice sticky. Sushi rice and sweet rice are high in amylopectin.
- Amylose is a longer type of starch that doesn't bind or stick together.

It is the balance of these two elements that defines whether the rice grains stick together or each grain cooks up separately.

The following also affect cooking times and the nature of the finished product.

- **Grain length/starch quantity:** Rice is distinguished by the length of the grain and the dominant type of starch in it. Some rice like basmati is long and skinny and contains amylose. Other rice like sushi, jasmine, or brown rice is short and fat and contains amylopectin.
- **Color:** Rice can be black, brown, white, or red. Each type has a distinct texture and flavor.
- **Aroma:** Basmati rice has kind of a popcorn aroma, jasmine has a floral aroma, and brown rice has a great nutty scent.

The different types of rice aren't always interchangeable and can't be swapped out for one another.

◂ Brown Rice

▴ Forbidden Rice

▸ Quinoa

▾ Wild Blend

▴ Sweet Rice

◂ Buckwheat

▸ Millet

◂ Farro

▸ Barley

▸ Basmati

Different Types of Rice

Here are a few guidelines to help you pick the correct type of rice for your dish. These are just guidelines, not rules, so at the end of the day, use whatever you like and enjoy it!

- **Basmati rice** doesn't get fatter as it cooks; it gets thinner and longer. I wish I were like this after a few cupcakes too many!
- **Jasmine rice** is a sticky rice, which means it forms small clumps, making it easy to eat with chopsticks.
- **Brown rice** is believed to be healthier, but it's really not that much healthier. Brown rice is all-purpose rice and usually tastes nuttier and chewier.
- **Black rice** has a coating that contains the same chemical as eggplant. This chemical gives black rice and the eggplant their color.
- **Sushi rice** is very sticky, which is why it's great for sushi rolls.
- **Glutinous rice** is not high in gluten, as the name might suggest. It's just really sticky (and yummy).

Choosing the Right Type of Rice

As you can see from the list, you should choose the type of rice depending on the dish you're making.

When you're making an Indian or Middle Eastern dish like biryani or pilau, you'll want basmati or long-grain to ensure that the grains will separate and not clump together.

On the other hand, if you're making Asian dishes that you would eat with chopsticks and need the rice to be a little sticky, you should choose jasmine. I also love jasmine rice with Thai curries when I cook with coconut milk, as the jasmine rice and coconut flavors pair so well together.

Brown rice is nutty and chewy and a good all-purpose rice. Traditionally, it's been considered healthier than white rice, but that's debatable, since it has only a little more fiber and can carry more contaminants if it's not organic. But it cooks really well in a pressure cooker, so it's fine to use as an all-purpose rice if you prefer the taste or texture to white rice.

Black rice, once known as "forbidden rice" because it was so extravagant only royalty ate it, has a bran hull that gives it its dark purple color. This rice is used for puddings and is quite sticky once you break the hull on the rice. Stickier kinds of rice like this have the ability to raise your blood sugar more than a longer-grain, less-sticky rice like basmati would.

Sushi rice is very sticky and starchy due to its high level of amylopectin. If you're watching your blood sugar, please note that the starchier the rice, the more it will raise it—so this one might be one to avoid.

Glutinous rice such as Arborio ironically has no gluten in it. This rice is the stickiest and is used for dishes such as puddings or risotto.

Out of all these rices, each one has a different type of starch and different levels of starch, which is the most important aspect to note.

Long-, Medium-, and Short-Grain Rice

Long-grain rice grows to about four times its length when cooked. Medium-grain rice grows about two times its size, and short-grain rice stays short and plumps up when cooking.

Why Pressure-Cook Rice?

Now that we've discussed how to pick the best rice for your dish, let's discuss why you should cook it in a pressure cooker.

Rice tastes so much different and better in the pressure cooker than in stovetop methods, but you don't want to just take your stovetop method and put it into a pressure cooker. The pressure cooker changes the chemistry of food and how the food reacts as it cooks. The pressure cooker prepares rice in a much different way than it would on the stove.

1. **Creamier mouthfeel:** The heat and moisture in a pressure cooker gelatinize the starch in rice for a much creamier mouthfeel. For basmati, which shouldn't get creamy, it cooks the rice the whole way through for nicely separated rice.

2. **Better aroma:** Cooking rice in a pressure cooker requires less water because there is no water being evaporated as there is in the stovetop method. One of the key benefits of cooking in a pressure cooker is that none of the aroma of the rice is lost and it turns out so much more flavorful.

3. **Hands-free:** You don't have to babysit rice in the pressure cooker, nor do you have to presoak the rice, resulting in less time and effort for you.

How Much Water to Use When Making Rice

It may surprise you to know that for all rice other than black and Arborio, the ratio of water to rice is 1:1. For Arborio and black rice, the ratio will be 1 cup rice and 1.5 cups water.

With brown, red, and mixed rice, the water and rice ratios remain the same, but the natural pressure release time needs to be 22 minutes, not just 10. I know that we were all taught differently, but remember that pressure cooking is much different than stovetop cooking.

Why Is It So Different and Why Is It So Much Quicker?

Because you don't lose water to evaporation in pressure cooking, you don't need more water for the more fibrous rice like brown rice.

However, different types of rice do require different cooking times because the water needs more time to penetrate the outer husk for brown, black, and red rice.

Be sure to be patient and let the steam release naturally when your rice is done because that's actually time that the rice is cooking. If you quick-release the cooker, the rice won't be cooked all the way through.

It's important to note that for all rice, I recommend rinsing it and draining off all the water prior to putting it in the pressure cooker.

Troubleshooting Rice in a Pressure Cooker

Of course, not everyone likes their rice exactly the same way, and mistakes can always occur in cooking, so below is a list of how to handle it if the rice doesn't turn out exactly the way you want it to:

- If the rice is too mushy, reduce the water then, if need be, reduce the time.
- If it's too chewy, try increasing the cooking time first, and if that doesn't work, try increasing the liquid.
- If the center of the rice is hard but the outer portion isn't, try increasing the water by a tad and, if need be, increase the cooking time.
- Always ensure you're doing a ten-minute NPR (natural pressure release).
- If the rice is sticking to the bottom, try adding ghee or butter first, then reduce the cooking and NPR time or try using a ceramic liner.

PESTO LENTILS AND RICE WITH TOMATOES

I had leftover pesto after making the Tomato-Pesto Soup (page 51) and decided to add it to the rice. So good! Instant flavor. The red lentils add nice texture and a little protein into the dish, and the cheese on top is wonderfully salty against the rice.

ACTIVE TIME	FUNCTION	RELEASE	TOTAL TIME
5 minutes	Manual (High)	Natural/Quick	30 minutes

Egg-Free • Gluten-Free • Soy-Free • Vegetarian • 30 Minutes or Less • Dairy-Free • SERVES 4 as a main dish

1 cup basmati rice, rinsed and drained

½ cup red lentils

½ cup diced onion

3 tablespoons pesto

1 teaspoon black pepper

½ teaspoon kosher salt

1¼ cups water

1 cup diced tomatoes

½ cup shredded Parmesan (optional)

1. In the Instant Pot, combine the rice, lentils, onion, pesto, pepper, salt, and water.

2. Secure the lid on the pot. Close the pressure-release valve. Select MANUAL and set the pot at HIGH pressure for 4 minutes. At the end of the cooking time, allow the pot to sit undisturbed for 10 minutes, then release any remaining pressure.

3. Gently mix in the tomatoes and Parmesan, if desired, and serve.

PER SERVING
Calories: 300
Total Fat: 5g
Saturated Fat: 1g
Sodium: 390mg
Carbohydrates: 53g
Fiber: 5g
Sugars: 2g
Protein: 10g

APPLESAUCE GRITS

I had to make these a few times to get the proportions right, but I got there eventually. I tried this with bits of apple and it really didn't work as well, so I'd say to stick with the applesauce.

ACTIVE TIME	FUNCTION	RELEASE	TOTAL TIME
5 minutes	Manual (High)	Natural/Quick	35 minutes

Egg-Free • Nut-Free • Gluten-Free • Soy-Free • Vegetarian • SERVES 4 as a side dish

Butter, for greasing the pan

1 cup old-fashioned grits

1 cup applesauce

1 cup raisins

1½ teaspoons apple pie spice or cinnamon

¼ teaspoon kosher salt

2 cups water, divided

1 tablespoon butter, diced

Optional toppings:
whole milk or full-fat coconut milk, chopped toasted nuts, brown sugar, and honey or maple syrup

1. Grease a 6 × 3-inch round heatproof pan with some butter.

2. In a medium bowl, combine the grits, applesauce, raisins, apple pie spice, salt, and ½ cup of the water. Pour the grits mixture into the prepared pan and scatter the diced butter on top.

3. Pour the remaining 1½ cups water into the Instant Pot. Place a trivet in the pot. Set the pan on the trivet.

4. Secure the lid on the pot. Close the pressure-release valve. Select MANUAL and set the pot at HIGH pressure for 10 minutes. At the end of the cooking time, allow the pot to sit undisturbed for 10 minutes, then release any remaining pressure.

5. Scoop into bowls, top with optional toppings, if desired, and serve.

PER SERVING

Calories: 320
Total Fat: 4g
Saturated Fat: 2g
Sodium: 150mg
Carbohydrates: 71g
Fiber: 3g
Sugars: 30g
Protein: 5g

BACON-BARLEY PILAF

If you prefer a lower-fat option, you can use chopped ham rather than bacon in this recipe, but in that case, add a little bit of oil or butter to the barley.

ACTIVE TIME	FUNCTION	RELEASE	TOTAL TIME
15 minutes	Sauté (Normal); Manual (High)	Natural/Quick	50 minutes

Egg-Free • Nut-Free • Dairy-Free • Gluten-Free • Soy-Free • SERVES 4 as a side dish

4 slices of bacon, chopped

2 cups diced mushrooms

1 cup diced onion

1¼ cups water, divided

1 cup pearled barley

1 teaspoon dried marjoram

1 teaspoon kosher salt

1 teaspoon black pepper

PER SERVING

Calories: 320
Total Fat: 12g
Saturated Fat: 4g
Sodium: 670mg
Carbohydrates: 44g
Fiber: 9g
Sugars: 3g
Protein: 10g

1. Select SAUTÉ/Normal on the Instant Pot. When the pot is hot, add the bacon. Cook, stirring frequently, until the bacon has rendered some fat, about 2 minutes. Add the mushrooms and onion and cook, stirring frequently, until the onion is softened and browned at the edges, 5 to 6 minutes.

2. Add ¼ cup of the water to deglaze the pot, scraping up the browned bits. Allow the water to evaporate entirely.

3. Add the barley, the remaining 1 cup water, marjoram, salt, and pepper. Stir to combine.

4. Secure the lid on the pot. Close the pressure-release valve. Select MANUAL and set the pot at HIGH pressure for 15 minutes. At the end of the cooking time, allow the pot to sit undisturbed for 10 minutes, then release any remaining pressure.

5. Fluff with a fork and serve.

BARLEY AND MUNG BEAN PILAF

I rarely write recipes with something you only use once in a cookbook. So, check out the Mung Beans with Turnip Greens recipe as well (page 175). But this pilaf is great with harissa-rubbed grilled meats (page 222 for the Harissa recipe) and is very hearty and filling.

ACTIVE TIME	FUNCTION	RELEASE	TOTAL TIME
5 minutes	Manual (High)	Natural/Quick	45 minutes

Egg-Free • Nut-Free • Dairy-Free • Gluten-Free • Soy-Free • Vegan • SERVES 6 as a side dish

1 cup pearled barley

¼ cup dried green mung beans

1 tablespoon vegetable oil

1 teaspoon kosher salt

1 teaspoon black pepper

½ teaspoon ground cinnamon

½ teaspoon allspice

¼ teaspoon nutmeg

1¼ cups water

Optional toppings:
Shredded Parmesan cheese, chopped parsley, toasted pine nuts

1. In the Instant Pot, combine the barley, mung beans, oil, salt, pepper, cinnamon, allspice, nutmeg, and water. Mix well.

2. Secure the lid on the pot. Close the pressure-release valve. Select MANUAL and set the pot at HIGH pressure for 15 minutes. At the end of the cooking time, allow the pot to sit undisturbed for 15 minutes, then release any remaining pressure.

3. Fluff with a fork and serve with optional toppings, if desired.

PER SERVING

Calories: 170
Total Fat: 3g
Saturated Fat: 0g
Sodium: 320mg
Carbohydrates: 31g
Fiber: 7g
Sugars: 1g
Protein: 5g

BARLEY-CHICKEN STEW

The turmeric adds a lovely hint of flavor and a warming yellow color to the broth. This soup just looks warm and welcoming. It's fantastic for an easy weeknight dinner.

ACTIVE TIME	FUNCTION	RELEASE	TOTAL TIME
10 minutes	Manual (High)	Natural/Quick	40 minutes

Egg-Free • Nut-Free • Dairy-Free • Gluten-Free • Soy-Free • SERVES 4 as a main dish

1 pound skinless bone-in chicken thighs

1 cup diced onion

1 cup thick carrot sticks (about 3 inches long)

½ cup medium pearled barley

1 teaspoon ground turmeric

1 teaspoon kosher salt

1 teaspoon black pepper

3 cups low-sodium chicken broth

½ cup chopped fresh parsley

1. In the Instant Pot, combine the chicken, onion, carrots, barley, turmeric, salt, pepper, and broth.

2. Secure the lid on the pot. Close the pressure-release valve. Select MANUAL and set the pot at HIGH pressure for 15 minutes. At the end of the cooking time, allow the pot to sit undisturbed for 5 minutes, then release any remaining pressure.

3. Remove the chicken from the bones and shred. Stir the shredded chicken into the pot.

4. Sprinkle with parsley and serve.

PER SERVING
Calories: 270
Total Fat: 8g
Saturated Fat: 2g
Sodium: 610mg
Carbohydrates: 29g
Fiber: 6g
Sugars: 4g
Protein: 23g

BROWN RICE AND LENTIL CASSEROLE

I had to test this a few times to get the water proportions right. We ate a lot of soupy brown rice and lentils that week! I often say that my motto should be "I curse when I cook so you don't have to." I hope you will hear nothing but words of appreciation when you make these.

ACTIVE TIME	FUNCTION	RELEASE	TOTAL TIME
10 minutes	Sauté (Normal); Manual (High)	Natural/Quick	55 minutes

Egg-Free · Nut-Free · Dairy-Free · Gluten-Free · Soy-Free · Vegan · SERVES 6 as a main dish

2 tablespoons vegetable oil

3 cloves garlic, minced

1 jalapeño, seeded if desired, minced

1 cup chopped onion

1 cup chopped tomatoes

1 cup brown basmati rice, rinsed and drained

¾ cup lentils

2 tablespoons salt-free taco seasoning

1½ teaspoons kosher salt

1¾ cups water

½ cup chopped green onions

½ cup chopped fresh cilantro or parsley

1. Select SAUTÉ/Normal on the Instant Pot. When the pot is hot, add the oil. Once the oil is hot, add the garlic and jalapeño and let sizzle for 15 seconds. Add the onion, tomatoes, rice, lentils, taco seasoning, salt, and water.

2. Secure the lid on the pot. Close the pressure-release valve. Select MANUAL and set the pot at HIGH pressure for 22 minutes. At the end of the cooking time, allow the pot to sit undisturbed for 10 minutes, then release any remaining pressure.

3. Garnish with green onions and cilantro and serve.

PER SERVING

Calories: 240
Total Fat: 6g
Saturated Fat: 1g
Sodium: 480mg
Carbohydrates: 40g
Fiber: 5g
Sugars: 3g
Protein: 9g

CRANBERRY-WALNUT PILAF

You can also use dried cherries rather than cranberries. I love to use toasted pine nuts rather than walnuts for a change.

ACTIVE TIME	FUNCTION	RELEASE	TOTAL TIME
10 minutes	Manual (High)	Natural/Quick	35 minutes

Egg-Free • Dairy-Free • Gluten-Free • Soy-Free • Vegan • SERVES 6 as a side dish

1 cup basmati rice, rinsed and drained

1 cup dried cranberries

1 cup grated carrots

1 cup water

1 teaspoon vegetable oil

½ teaspoon kosher salt

2 strands saffron, crushed (optional)

1 cup chopped walnuts, toasted

PER SERVING
Calories: 300
Total Fat: 14g
Saturated Fat: 2g
Sodium: 170mg
Carbohydrates: 43g
Fiber: 4g
Sugars: 15g
Protein: 5g

1. In the Instant Pot, combine the rice, cranberries, carrots, water, oil, salt, and saffron, if using.

2. Secure the lid on the pot. Close the pressure-release valve. Select MANUAL and set the pot at HIGH pressure for 4 minutes. At the end of the cooking time, allow the pot to sit undisturbed for 10 minutes, then release any remaining pressure.

3. Scatter the walnuts over the rice and serve.

FARRO-APPLE SALAD

This is a good sweet-and-savory salad, and the blue cheese makes it taste really fancy, yet it's very easy to make. You could use pears instead of apples for this, and I've been known to throw in the odd grape or two from time to time.

ACTIVE TIME	FUNCTION	RELEASE	TOTAL TIME
15 minutes	Manual (High)	Natural/Quick	50 minutes plus 15 minutes soaking time

Egg-Free • Soy-Free • Vegetarian • SERVES 4 as a main dish; 6 as a side dish

For the Farro

1 cup pearled farro

2 cups water

5 cups chopped fresh kale

For the Dressing

½ cup Greek yogurt

2 tablespoons chopped fresh parsley

1 to 2 tablespoons honey or maple syrup

1 tablespoon fresh lemon juice

1 teaspoon kosher salt

½ teaspoon black pepper

For Finishing

2 cups chopped apples or pears

½ cup blue cheese crumbles

½ cup toasted pecan halves

½ cup raisins

1. **For the Farro:** Place the farro in a medium bowl. Cover with hot water and soak for 15 to 20 minutes; drain.

2. In the Instant Pot, combine the farro and water.

3. Secure the lid on the pot. Close the pressure-release valve. Select MANUAL and set the pot at HIGH pressure for 8 minutes. At the end of the cooking time, allow the pot to sit undisturbed for 10 minutes, then release any remaining pressure.

4. Open the lid, and stir in the kale. Close the lid, and let the kale cook in the residual heat, about 5 minutes; drain and rinse with cool water.

5. **For the Dressing:** In a large mixing bowl, whisk together the yogurt, parsley, honey, lemon juice, salt, and pepper.

6. **For Finishing:** Add the farro mixture, apples, blue cheese, pecans, and raisins to the bowl with the dressing; toss to thoroughly combine.

PER SERVING		
Calories: 480	Sodium: 690mg	Sugars: 27g
Total Fat: 18g	Carbohydrates: 69g	Protein: 15g
Saturated Fat: 6g	Fiber: 10g	

FARRO RISOTTO WITH GOAT CHEESE

Farro makes such a wonderful creamy risotto. I created a few different farro recipes for my *Instant Pot Miracle Vegetarian* cookbook and realized how versatile it could be. I find it a lot more filling than rice, so it's great as a hearty side or main dish.

ACTIVE TIME	FUNCTION	RELEASE	TOTAL TIME
10 minutes	Sauté (Normal); Manual (High)	Natural/Quick	1 hour 10 minutes

Egg-Free • Nut-Free • Soy-Free • Vegetarian • SERVES 4 as a main dish; 6 as a side dish

1 cup pearled farro

1 tablespoon butter or vegetable oil

3 cloves garlic, minced

1¼ cups chopped green onions (green and white parts), divided

1½ cups water

1 teaspoon kosher salt

1 teaspoon black pepper

½ teaspoon dried thyme

4 ounces semi-soft goat cheese, crumbled

1 cup frozen peas, thawed

PER SERVING

Calories: 360
Total Fat: 14g
Saturated Fat: 9g
Sodium: 650mg
Carbohydrates: 43g
Fiber: 8g
Sugars: 3g
Protein: 18g

1. Place the farro in a medium bowl. Cover with hot water and soak for 15 to 20 minutes; drain.

2. Select SAUTÉ/Normal on the Instant Pot. When the pot is hot, add the butter. Once the butter is melted, add the garlic and allow it to sizzle for 5 to 10 seconds. Add 1 cup of the green onions and stir. Select CANCEL.

3. Add the farro, water, salt, pepper, and thyme. Scatter the goat cheese on top. Do not stir.

4. Secure the lid on the pot. Close the pressure-release valve. Select MANUAL and set the pot at HIGH pressure for 10 minutes. At the end of the cooking time, allow the pot to sit undisturbed for 10 minutes, then release any remaining pressure.

5. Open the lid, add the peas, and stir until ingredients are well combined. Close the lid, and allow the peas to cook in the residual heat, about 5 minutes.

6. Garnish with the remaining ¼ cup green onions and serve.

JOLLOF RICE

My followers have been asking for a jollof rice recipe for two years now. This one is very easy to make and tastes very authentic. I've used leftovers in a cold salad as well.

ACTIVE TIME	FUNCTION	RELEASE	TOTAL TIME
15 minutes	Manual (High)	Natural/Quick	40 minutes

Egg-Free • Nut-Free • Dairy-Free • Gluten-Free • Soy-Free • Vegan • SERVES 4 as a side dish

1 cup diced tomatoes

1 cup stemmed, seeded, and roughly chopped bell pepper (any color)

1 cup basmati rice, rinsed and drained

½ cup diced onion

2 tablespoons vegetable oil

3 cloves garlic, minced

1 tablespoon minced fresh ginger

2 teaspoons dried thyme

1 teaspoon smoked paprika

1 teaspoon kosher salt

1 teaspoon curry powder

1 bay leaf

1 cup water

2 tablespoons tomato paste

1. In the Instant Pot, combine the tomatoes, bell pepper, rice, onion, oil, garlic, ginger, thyme, paprika, salt, curry powder, bay leaf, and water. (Make sure that the rice is under the liquid. This is to ensure that the rice cooks evenly.) Place the tomato paste in dollops over the rice.

2. Secure the lid on the pot. Close the pressure-release valve. Select MANUAL and set the pot at HIGH pressure for 4 minutes. At the end of the cooking time, allow the pot to sit undisturbed for 10 minutes, then release any remaining pressure.

3. Discard the bay leaf, stir well to combine, and serve.

PER SERVING

Calories: 160
Total Fat: 7g
Saturated Fat: 1g
Sodium: 490mg
Carbohydrates: 23g
Fiber: 2g
Sugars: 3g
Protein: 3g

KASHA PILAF WITH MUSHROOMS

I used to make this pilaf when my older son was a baby, oh, twenty-eight years ago! I don't know why I stopped making it, but here it is again in all its former glory. Mushrooms add a ton of flavor and stay intact even through longer pressure cooking.

ACTIVE TIME	FUNCTION	RELEASE	TOTAL TIME
15 minutes	Sauté (High); Manual (High)	Natural/Quick	50 minutes

Egg-Free • Nut-Free • Dairy-Free • Gluten-Free • Soy-Free • Vegan • SERVES 4 as a side dish

2 tablespoons vegetable oil

1 cup chopped onion

2 cups chopped mushrooms

1¼ cups water, divided

1 cup toasted buckwheat groats (kasha)

1 teaspoon kosher salt

½ teaspoon black pepper

PER SERVING

Calories: 230
Total Fat: 8g
Saturated Fat: 1g
Sodium: 490mg
Carbohydrates: 36g
Fiber: 5g
Sugars: 2g
Protein: 6g

1. Select SAUTÉ/High on the Instant Pot. When the pot is hot, add the oil. Once the oil is hot, add the onion and cook, stirring frequently, until the edges are browned, 3 to 4 minutes. Stir in the mushrooms.

2. Add ¼ cup of the water to deglaze the pot, scraping up the browned bits. Allow the water to evaporate completely. Add the buckwheat groats, salt, pepper, and the remaining 1 cup water.

3. Secure the lid on the pot. Close the pressure-release valve. Select MANUAL and set the pot at HIGH pressure for 15 minutes. At the end of the cooking time, allow the pot to sit undisturbed for 10 minutes, then release any remaining pressure.

4. Fluff with a fork and serve.

QUINOA AND EDAMAME SALAD

Here's another example of how to use your Instant Pot to create salads that are crisp and crunchy. That peanut dressing is the shining star of this recipe. It keeps well in the refrigerator for a week, so make extra and enjoy.

ACTIVE TIME	FUNCTION	RELEASE	TOTAL TIME
20 minutes	Manual (High)	Natural/Quick	40 minutes

Egg-Free • Dairy-Free • Vegan • SERVES 4 as a main dish; 6 as a side dish

For the Dressing

2 tablespoons hot water

2 tablespoons peanut butter

2 tablespoons apple cider vinegar

2 teaspoons minced fresh ginger

1 tablespoon soy sauce

½ teaspoon kosher salt

For the Quinoa

1 cup quinoa, rinsed and drained

1 cup shelled edamame

1 cup water

1 cup stemmed, seeded, and roughly chopped red and yellow bell peppers

1 cup cherry tomatoes, halved

1 cup shredded carrots

½ teaspoon kosher salt

½ cup chopped fresh cilantro (optional)

1. **For the Dressing:** In a large mixing bowl, combine the hot water and peanut butter and whisk until smooth. Add the vinegar, ginger, soy sauce, and salt. Whisk until smooth.

2. **For the Quinoa:** In the Instant Pot, combine the quinoa, edamame, and water.

3. Secure the lid on the pot. Close the pressure-release valve. Select MANUAL and set the pot at HIGH pressure for 1 minute. At the end of the cooking time, allow the pot to sit undisturbed for 5 minutes, then release any remaining pressure.

4. Drain the quinoa and edamame and rinse under cold water.

5. Add the quinoa and edamame, bell peppers, cherry tomatoes, carrots, and salt to the bowl with the dressing. Toss to combine.

6. Garnish with cilantro, if desired, and serve.

PER SERVING

Calories: 310
Total Fat: 9g
Saturated Fat: 1g
Sodium: 860mg
Carbohydrates: 41g
Fiber: 15g
Sugars: 7g
Protein: 14g

SAN FRANCISCO RICE

Yup, I recreated Rice-A-Roni—except since it's homemade, you can control the sodium in it, which is where the box mix stumbles a little nutritionally. It's pretty, it's easy, it's delicious.

ACTIVE TIME	FUNCTION	RELEASE	TOTAL TIME
10 minutes	Sauté (High); Manual (High)	Natural/Quick	35 minutes

Egg-Free • Nut-Free • Dairy-Free • Soy-Free • Vegan • SERVES 6 as a side dish

2 teaspoons dried parsley

1 teaspoon kosher salt

½ teaspoon garlic powder

½ teaspoon ground turmeric

2 tablespoons vegetable oil

½ cup broken fideo or angel hair pasta (1 ounce)

¾ cup long-grain white rice, rinsed and drained

½ cup chopped onion

1⅓ cups chicken broth, water, or low-sodium vegetable broth

½ to 1 cup frozen mixed vegetables (optional, see Note)

½ cup shredded Parmesan cheese (optional)

PER SERVING

Calories: 160
Total Fat: 5g
Saturated Fat: 1g
Sodium: 340mg
Carbohydrates: 26g
Fiber: 1g
Sugars: 1g
Protein: 4g

1. In a small bowl, combine the parsley, salt, garlic powder, and turmeric. Stir until well combined.

2. Select SAUTÉ/High on the Instant Pot. When the pot is hot, add the oil. Once the oil is hot, add the pasta, and cook, stirring frequently, until the pasta is browned, about 5 minutes.

3. Add the rice, onion, and spice mixture and stir well. Add the broth.

4. Scatter the vegetables on top, if using. Do not stir.

5. Secure the lid on the pot. Close the pressure-release valve. Select MANUAL and set the pot at HIGH pressure for 4 minutes. At the end of the cooking time, allow the pot to sit undisturbed for 10 minutes, then release any remaining pressure.

6. Stir in the Parmesan cheese, if using, and serve.

NOTE: If you'd like to add vegetables to this, you can scatter a cup of frozen corn or frozen carrots and peas on top. Do not use fresh vegetables, as they will overcook, and do not use more than 1 cup of veggies, otherwise your proportions for water will be off.

TACO RICE-AND-BEAN CASSEROLE

This is a super family-friendly meal. Using just half a pound of meat and adding red beans lets you reduce the meat without losing the heartiness and has the added benefit of using plant protein to round out your meal. You can garnish with cheese, cilantro, avocados, sour cream—whatever your taste buds and dietary considerations allow.

ACTIVE TIME	FUNCTION	RELEASE	TOTAL TIME
15 minutes	Sauté (Normal); Manual (High)	Natural/Quick	40 minutes

Egg-Free · Nut-Free · Dairy-Free · Gluten-Free · Soy-Free · SERVES 4 as a main dish

8 ounces (90% lean) ground beef

1 cup diced onion

1¼ cups water, divided

3 tablespoons salt-free taco seasoning

1½ teaspoons kosher salt

1 cup basmati rice, rinsed and drained

1 cup diced fresh tomatoes

1 cup stemmed, seeded, and roughly chopped bell peppers (any color)

1 (14.5-ounce) can kidney beans, rinsed and drained, or 1½ cups cooked kidney beans

Optional toppings:
shredded cheddar cheese or shredded Mexican blend cheese, chopped cilantro, diced avocado, sour cream, or salsa

1. Select SAUTÉ/Normal on the Instant Pot. When the pot is hot, add the ground beef and onion and cook, breaking up the meat with a wooden spoon, for 3 to 5 minutes. Add ¼ cup of the water to deglaze the pot, scraping up the browned bits. Allow the water to evaporate completely. Add the taco seasoning, salt, and rice and mix thoroughly.

2. Add the remaining 1 cup water. Scatter the tomatoes, bell peppers, and beans on top of the rice and meat mixture. Do not stir.

3. Secure the lid on the pot. Close the pressure-release valve. Select MANUAL and set the pot at HIGH pressure for 4 minutes. At the end of the cooking time, allow the pot to sit undisturbed for 10 minutes, then release any remaining pressure.

4. Stir to combine and serve with optional toppings, if desired.

PER SERVING

Calories: 340
Total Fat: 6g
Saturated Fat: 2g
Sodium: 990mg
Carbohydrates: 52g
Fiber: 6g
Sugars: 5g
Protein: 19g

WILD RICE BLEND PILAF WITH VEGETABLES AND PINE NUTS

Here's another "could be a hot side dish, could be a cold salad" recipe. Use the preblended wild rice mix rather than mixing your own. The blends contain parboiled brown rice so that everything cooks at the same time.

ACTIVE TIME	FUNCTION	RELEASE	TOTAL TIME
10 minutes	Manual (High)	Natural/Quick	1 hour

Egg-Free • Dairy-Free • Gluten-Free • Soy-Free • Vegan • SERVES 6 as a side dish

1 cup wild rice blend

1 tablespoon vegetable oil

2 teaspoons dried basil

1 teaspoon kosher salt

½ teaspoon red pepper flakes

1 cup water

4 cups chopped spinach

1 cup stemmed, seeded, and roughly chopped bell pepper (any color)

1 cup chopped tomatoes

¼ cup toasted pine nuts or other nuts

1. In the Instant Pot, combine the rice, oil, basil, salt, red pepper flakes, and water. Stir well.

2. Secure the lid on the pot. Close the pressure-release valve. Select MANUAL and set the pot at HIGH pressure for 25 minutes. At the end of the cooking time, allow the pot to sit undisturbed for 15 minutes, then release any remaining pressure.

3. Open the lid, and stir in the spinach, bell pepper, and tomatoes. Close the lid and allow the vegetables to cook in the residual heat for 5 minutes.

4. Stir in toasted nuts and serve.

PER SERVING

Calories: 140
Total Fat: 4g
Saturated Fat: 0g
Sodium: 340mg
Carbohydrates: 27g
Fiber: 3g
Sugars: 1g
Protein: 3g

SAUCES AND SPICE MIXES

CAJUN SPICE

You can certainly use a store-bought Cajun mix, but I like making it at home so I can play with the proportions. I like to add more cayenne than what I have listed here, so you can always use more (or less!) than the 1 teaspoon.

ACTIVE TIME	TOTAL TIME
5 minutes	5 minutes

Suitable for all diets • 30 Minutes or Less • MAKES about 4 tablespoons

1 teaspoon dried oregano

1 teaspoon dried thyme

1 tablespoon dried parsley flakes

1 tablespoon dehydrated minced onion

1 teaspoon dehydrated minced garlic

1 tablespoon smoked paprika

1 teaspoon cayenne pepper

1 teaspoon black pepper

1 teaspoon salt

In a small bowl, stir together the oregano, thyme, parsley flakes, onion, garlic, paprika, cayenne pepper, black pepper, and salt. Store in an airtight container in a cool, dark place for up to 2 months.

GARAM MASALA

This garam masala is the base of much of my Indian cooking. I've tried many different blends, but this is Raghavan Iyer's recipe (he of *660 Curries* fame), and he has been generous enough to allow me and all who cook from my recipes to use this. Everyone who has tried it will agree—store-bought garam masala cannot hold a candle to this. Take my advice—take the ten minutes it takes to make this. You will thank me.

ACTIVE TIME	TOTAL TIME
10 minutes	10 minutes

Suitable for all diets · 30 Minutes or Less · MAKES about 4 tablespoons

2 tablespoons coriander seeds

1 teaspoon cumin seeds

½ teaspoon whole cloves

½ teaspoon cardamom seeds from green/white pods

2 dried bay leaves

3 dried red chiles or ½ teaspoon cayenne pepper or red pepper flakes

1 (2-inch) piece cinnamon/cassia bark

1. Combine coriander seeds, cumin seeds, cloves, cardamom seeds, bay leaves, chiles, and cinnamon in a clean coffee or spice grinder. Grind, shaking as it's being ground, so all the seeds and bits get into the blades, until mixture has the consistency of a moderately fine powder.

2. Unplug the grinder and turn it upside down. (You want all the spice mixture to collect in the lid so you can easily scoop it out without cutting yourself playing about the blades.)

3. Store in an airtight container in a cool, dark place. Shake or stir before using.

HARISSA

Many harissa recipes use tomatoes or peppers. I prefer my paste to be straight-up spice. Taste it once and you will find a million different uses for this lovely, spicy, versatile mix.

ACTIVE TIME	TOTAL TIME
5 minutes	10 minutes

Suitable for all diets · 30 Minutes or Less · MAKES about ¾ cup

½ cup vegetable oil

6 cloves garlic, minced

2 tablespoons smoked paprika

1 tablespoon ground coriander

1 tablespoon ground cumin

1 teaspoon ground caraway

1 teaspoon kosher salt

½ to 1 teaspoon cayenne pepper

1. In a medium microwave-safe bowl, combine the oil, garlic, paprika, coriander, cumin, caraway, salt, and cayenne. Microwave on high for 1 minute, stirring halfway through the cooking time. (You can also heat this on the stovetop until the oil is hot and bubbling.)

2. Cool completely. Store in an airtight container in the refrigerator for up to 1 month.

GHEE

I don't understand why it's so expensive to buy ghee in stores because it's fairly idiot-proof to make at home. And it keeps forever on your countertop in a sealed container—or, at least, it keeps as long as it takes for you to devour it . . . which isn't very long at our house.

ACTIVE TIME	TOTAL TIME
5 minutes	35 minutes

Egg-Free • Nut-Free • Gluten-Free • Grain-Free • Soy-Free • Vegetarian • Low-Carb • MAKES 2 cups

1 pound (4 sticks) unsalted butter

1. Place the butter in a heavy-bottomed saucepan over medium-low heat. Set a timer for 20 minutes and leave it alone! Don't stir the butter or mess with it in any way. Just let it be. During this time, the water from the butter will evaporate. You'll see a light foam forming on top. It will sound like popcorn popping—but much softer.

2. At the 20-minute mark, stir the butter and raise the heat to medium-high. Cook, stirring occasionally, until you see the milk solids start turning brown and settling on the bottom of the pan. If you give up before this stage you are either (a) a quitter or (b) trying to make clarified butter, not ghee.

3. Let the mixture cool a little, then strain the clear yellow liquid through a fine-mesh strainer into a jar, and you're done. (Discard the browned milk solids.)

4. Seal the jar tightly with the lid. You can store the ghee on your countertop almost indefinitely, as long as you keep it sealed and use a clean spoon each time you dig into it.

CHART OF DIETARY CONSIDERATIONS	PAGE	EGG-FREE	NUT-FREE	DAIRY-FREE	GLUTEN-FREE
BEET AND YOGURT SALAD	33	X			X
BRAISED GREEN BEANS WITH HAM	34	X	X	X	X
BRAISED LEEKS	35	X	X	X	X
BRAISED LETTUCE WITH PEAS AND CARROTS	36	X	X		X
CABBAGE AND POTATO SOUP SHCHI	38	X	X		X
CREAMY SPICY GREENS	39	X	X	X	X
CREAMY TOMATO AND CARROT SOUP	40	X	X		X
CURRIED PUMPKIN SOUP	41	X	X	X	X
EDAMAME, CORN, AND COUSCOUS SALAD	43	X	X		
NAPA CABBAGE AND TOFU SOUP	44	X	X	X	
ROSEMARY GREEN BEANS AND TOMATOES	46	X	X	X	X
SPICED SWEET POTATOES	45	X			X
SPICY TOMATO-CHEESE GRITS	48	X	X		X
TOMATO-PESTO SOUP	51	X			
VEGAN CREAMED SPINACH	49	X	X	X	X
VEGETABLE AND COUSCOUS MEDLEY	52	X	X	X	
WILD RICE AND MUSHROOM SOUP	55	X	X		X
CAJUN-STYLE CHICKEN AND OKRA STEW	58	X	X	X	X
CHICKEN AND COUSCOUS SOUP	61	X	X	X	
CHICKEN AND POTATO CURRY	59	X	X	X	X
CHICKEN AND VEGETABLE STEW	62	X	X	X	X
CHICKEN POT PIE SOUP	65	X	X		X
CHICKEN TACO SALAD	66	X	X	X	X
CHICKEN TACO SOUP	69	X	X	X	X
CREAMY CHICKEN AND RICE	70	X	X		X
CREAMY CHICKEN SOUP	72	X	X		X
GINGERY CHICKEN SOUP WITH BOK CHOY AND SPINACH	73	X	X	X	X
GREEN ONION RICE WITH CORNISH GAME HEN AND EDAMAME	75	X	X	X	X
JERK CHICKEN AND QUINOA	76	X	X	X	X
LEMONY CHICKEN AND RICE SOUP	78	X	X	X	X
MEXICAN CHICKEN AND RICE SOUP	79	X	X	X	X
PEANUT BUTTER CHICKEN	80	X		X	
SAVORY BREAD PUDDING	81		X		
TURKEY AND KALE SOUP	84	X	X	X	X
WONTON-STYLE MEATBALL SOUP	83		X	X	
BEEF AND LEEK STEW	89	X	X	X	X

GRAIN-FREE	SOY-FREE	VEGETARIAN	VEGAN	LOW-CARB	30 Minutes or Less
X	X	X			
X	X			X	
X	X	X	X	X	X
X	X	X		X	X
X	X	X			
X	X	X	X	X	
X	X	X		X	
X	X	X			
		X			X
		X	X	X	X
X	X	X	X	X	X
X	X	X			X
	X	X			X
	X	X			
X		X	X	X	X
	X	X	X		X
X	X	X			
X	X				
	X				
X	X				
X	X				
X	X			X	
X	X			X	
X	X				
	X				
X	X			X	X
X	X			X	
	X				
	X				
	X				
				X	
	X				
X	X			X	X
				X	
	X				

CHART OF DIETARY CONSIDERATIONS	PAGE	EGG-FREE	NUT-FREE	DAIRY-FREE	GLUTEN-FREE	
BEEF, BARLEY, AND RICE SOUP	90	X	X	X		
BEEF DAUBE	92	X	X		X	
BEEF STROGANOFF	93	X	X			
BEEF TERIYAKI AND RICE	95	X	X	X		
BRAISED BEEF SHORT RIBS	98	X	X	X	X	
CHIPOTLE-ORANGE PORK	101	X	X	X	X	
CLASSIC POT ROAST	102	X	X	X		
HAM AND RICE WITH VEGETABLES	97	X	X	X		
HEARTY BEEF STEW	105	X	X	X		
IRISH LAMB STEW	106	X	X	X	X	
NEW ENGLAND BOILED DINNER	108	X	X	X	X	
ONE-POT BIBIMBAP	111	X	X	X		
PAPRIKA PORK CHOPS WITH CABBAGE	107	X	X		X	
PORK BELLY AND BOK CHOY NOODLE SOUP	114	X	X	X		
RENDANG-STYLE BEEF AND POTATOES	116	X	X	X	X	
SAUERKRAUT, POTATOES, AND SAUSAGE	113	X	X	X	X	
SAUSAGE, POTATO, AND KALE SOUP	119	X	X	X	X	
SHREDDED PORK TACOS	120	X	X	X	X	
SPICY BEEF BARBACOA	123	X	X	X	X	
SPLIT PEAS AND HAM	124	X	X	X	X	
SWEET-AND-SOUR STEAK AND CABBAGE STEW	126	X	X	X		
TEXAS-STYLE CHILI	129	X	X	X	X	
VIETNAMESE BEEF STEW	125	X	X	X	X	
WHITE BEAN AND SAUSAGE SOUP	130	X	X	X	X	
BELIZEAN COCONUT AND SEAFOOD SOUP	134	X	X	X	X	
CHIMICHURRI FISH AND COUSCOUS	135	X	X	X		
EASIEST-EVER SHRIMP CURRY	137	X	X	X	X	
FISH AND CHARD SOUP	138	X	X	X		
FISH AND CORN CHOWDER	141	X	X		X	
FISH AND POTATO SOUP WITH SOUR CREAM AND DILL	142	X	X		X	
HONEY-MUSTARD SALMON WITH RICE AND VEGETABLES	145	X	X	X		
PAPRIKA SPICED FISH AND VEGETABLE SOUP	146	X	X	X	X	
SALMON AND POTATO CURRY	149	X	X	X	X	
SALMON AND QUINOA SALAD	150	X	X	X	X	
THREE-INGREDIENT TOMATO LENTILS	160	X	X	X	X	
BLACK BEAN AND CHORIZO STEW	161	X	X	X	X	

GRAIN-FREE	SOY-FREE	VEGETARIAN	VEGAN	LOW-CARB	30 Minutes or Less
	x				
	x				
	x			x	
				x	
x	x			x	
x	x				x
	x				
x	x			x	
x	x			x	
x	x				
x	x			x	x
x	x				
x	x			x	
x	x			x	
x	x				
				x	x
	x			x	
	x				
x	x			x	
x	x			x	x
	x			x	x
	x			x	x
				x	x
	x				x
x	x			x	x
x	x			x	x
x	x			x	x
	x				x
	x				x
x	x		x		
x	x				

GRAIN-FREE	SOY-FREE	VEGETARIAN	VEGAN	LOW-CARB	30 Minutes or Less
x	x	x	x		
x	x	x	x		
x	x	x	x		
x	x	x	x		
x	x	x	x		
x	x	x	x		
x	x	x	x	x	
	x				x
x	x	x	x		
x	x	x	x		
x	x	x	x		
	x	x	x		
x		x	x		
	x	x			
	x				
	x	x	x		
	x				
	x	x	x		
	x	x	x		
	x	x			
	x	x			
	x	x	x		
	x	x	x		
	x	x			x
		x	x		
	x	x	x		
	x				
	x	x	x		
x	x	x	x	x	x
x	x	x	x	x	x
x	x	x		x	
x	x	x	x	x	x

INDEX

NOTE: Page references in *italics* refer to photos of recipes.

Need more easy weeknight recipes?

Don't miss these other great titles from Urvashi Pitre